# The Collapse of the Soviet Union: The History of the USSR Under Gorbachev

## By Charles River Editors

A picture of the Berlin Wall taken in 1990

## About Charles River Editors

**Charles River Editors** is a boutique digital publishing company, specializing in bringing history back to life with educational and engaging books on a wide range of topics. Keep up to date with our new and free offerings with this 5 second sign up on our weekly mailing list, and visit Our Kindle Author Page to see other recently published Kindle titles.

We make these books for you and always want to know our readers' opinions, so we encourage you to leave reviews and look forward to publishing new and exciting titles each week.

# Introduction

**President Gerald Ford and Brezhnev**

## The Collapse of the Soviet Union

For 30 years, much of the West looked on with disdain as the Bolsheviks took power in Russia and created and consolidated the Soviet Union. As bad as Vladimir Lenin seemed in the early 20th century, Joseph Stalin was so much worse that Churchill later remarked of Lenin, "Their worst misfortune was his birth... their next worst his death." Before World War II, Stalin consolidated his position by frequently purging party leaders (most famously Leon Trotsky) and Red Army leaders, executing hundreds of thousands of people at the least. And in one of history's greatest textbook examples of the idea that the enemy of my enemy is my friend, Stalin's Soviet Union allied with Britain and the United States to defeat Hitler in Europe during World War II.

A barely known figure outside of the Eastern bloc, Khrushchev was derided as a buffoon by one Western diplomat and mocked for his physical appearance by others, but any Western hopes that he would prove a more conciliatory figure than Stalin were quickly snuffed out as the hard-line Khrushchev embraced confrontational stances. In a statement to Western diplomats at the Polish embassy in Moscow, Khruschev famously warned, "We will bury you." And after his first meetings with President John F. Kennedy, Kennedy famously compared Khrushchev's negotiating techniques to his own father's. Even today, one of Khrushchev's most memorable moments is banging his shoe at a United Nations General Assembly meeting in September 1960 while a Filipino delegate was speaking.

Personal histrionics aside, Khrushchev meant business when dealing with the West, especially the United States and its young president, John F. Kennedy. After sensing weakness and a lack of fortitude in Kennedy, Khrushchev made his most audacious and ultimately costly decision by attempting to place nuclear warheads at advanced, offensive bases located in Cuba, right off the American mainland. As it turned out, the Cuban Missile Crisis would show the Kennedy Administration's resolve, force Khrushchev to back down, and ultimately sow the seeds of Khrushchev's fall from power. By the time he died in 1971, he had been declared a non-citizen of the nation he had ruled for nearly 20 years.

Leonid Brezhnev became First Secretary of the Communist Party in the Soviet Union in late 1964 after a plot to oust Khrushchev. Little is remembered in the public imagination about Brezhnev in comparison to Mikhail Gorbachev, Vladimir Lenin, or Joseph Stalin, despite the fact Brezhnev ruled the USSR from 1964-1982, longer than any Soviet leader other than Stalin. In fact, he held power during a tumultuous era that changed the world in remarkable ways, and that era has been favorably remembered by many former Soviet citizens. It marked a period of relative calm and even prosperity after the destruction of World War II and the tensions brought about by Khrushchev. Foremost amongst Brezhnev's achievements would be the détente period in the early 1970s, when the Soviets and Americans came to a number of agreements that reduced Cold War pressures and the alarming threat of nuclear war.

On the other side of the balance sheet, Brezhnev oversaw a malaise in Soviet society that later became known as an era of stagnation during which the Communist Bloc fell far behind the West in terms of economic output and standard of living. His regime also became notorious for its human rights abuses, and Soviet foreign policy in his later years took on some of the character of the earlier American behavior that he had so criticized. Most calamitous of all was the invasion of Afghanistan in 1979.

The Cold War moved into one of its most dangerous phases after Brezhnev's death as both sides deployed nuclear weapons within alarming proximity in Europe. A NATO exercise, "Operation Able Archer," almost led to a Soviet miscalculation, and when the Soviets shot down a South Korean airliner in September 1983, claiming it had strayed into Soviet airspace, the Cold War became very tense indeed.

After going through three elderly leaders in three years, Mikhail Gorbachev was chosen as the new General Secretary at the relatively youg age of 54 in March 1985. Gorbachev hoped to build the Soviet economy to relieve the persistent shortages of consumer goods it faced, which were caused by enormous military spending of the Soviet Union. Gorbachev tried to introduce some economic reforms, but they were blocked by communist hardliners. Gorbachev then came to the belief that the Soviet economy could not improved without political reform as well.

Limited political reforms, such as broadcasting uncensored debates in which politicians openly questioned government policy, backfired when they energized eastern European opposition movements which began to overthrow their communist governments in 1989. Gorbachev was unwilling to reoccupy these eastern European nations and use the Soviet army to put down these revolts.

Inspired by the revolts in Eastern Europe, the small Soviet Baltic republics, which had long chafed under Russian rule, also began to clamor for independence from the Soviet Union. In 1990, Gorbachev allowed non-Communist party politicians to run for office throughout the Soviet Union, and the Communist Party lost to independence candidates in six Soviet republics, including the three Baltic republics. The Baltic republics then declared independence from the Soviet Union.

In comparison with other Soviet leaders, Gorbachev was leader of the USSR for a relatively short period, but the changes that took place under his leadership were monumental, including some that were intended and others that were unforeseen. Gorbachev oversaw the end of the Cold War and the peaceful transition away from communism in Central and Eastern Europe, and he ended the war in Afghanistan and many other proxy conflicts in the developing world. Gorbachev improved relations with the West and developed enough trust with President Ronald Reagan and President George H.W. Bush to decommission thousands of nuclear weapons. He also liberalized the political environment within the Soviet Union itself, increased accountability, and brought in a certain degree of democracy.

Gorbachev was awarded the Nobel Peace Prize for these efforts in 1990, but his regime also left a legacy of turbulence and destruction in its wake. As a result of his policies, many Soviet people rose up against the status quo, demanding national self-determination and reviving old grievances. Gorbachev could not prevent the USSR from disbanding at the end of 1991, leaving much of the country's economy in ruins and nationalist and ethnic conflicts that are still unresolved today. Gorbachev was more popular abroad than he was at home, and in many respects, historians are still debating the costs and benefits of the last Soviet General Secretary's approach.

*The Collapse of the Soviet Union: The History of the USSR Under Mikhail Gorbachev* examines the final years of their empire, and how it all came crashing down in a relatively short period of time. Along with pictures of important people and places, you will learn about the collapse of the Soviet Union like never before.

The Collapse of the Soviet Union: The History of the USSR Under Mikhail Gorbachev

About Charles River Editors

Introduction

    Political Turbulence

    Gorbachev's Immediate Challenges

    Gorbachev's Tentative Domestic Reforms

    Gorbachev's Early Foreign Policy

    An Acceleration of Domestic Policies

    Crumbling Communism

    A New World Order

    Online Resources

    Bibliography

Free Books by Charles River Editors

Discounted Books by Charles River Editors

**Political Turbulence**

The Brezhnev regime had experienced challenges since coming to power in 1964, and it eventually sought some kind of accommodation – détente - with the West, if only to provide some breathing space before the next phase of the Cold War. At the same time, officials in Washington were urgently concerned with extricating American forces from Vietnam, giving both sides incentives to meet at a negotiating table.

**Brezhnev**

In some respects, Brezhnev was well-placed to reduce tensions with the United States. A jocular figure in person, Brezhnev was a compromise figure in the Soviet Politburo and therefore more secure of his position than someone like Nikita Khrushchev. His opposite number in 1968, however, was far less secure. President Lyndon B. Johnson had made a series of catastrophic escalations in the Vietnam War, leading to a huge death toll and catalyzing constant protests on American streets. Earlier that year, Johnson had announced that he would not campaign for reelection, but negotiations throughout 1968 prevented further progress for him when it came to ending the war.

Even as the Vietnam quagmire continued, Johnson managed to negotiate the Treaty on the Non-Proliferation of Nuclear Weapons (NPT) with the Soviets in July 1968. The NPT required signatories to renounce the use of nuclear weapons and only develop nuclear power for peaceful civilian purposes. The treaty allowed the two superpowers the opportunity to maintain the nuclear status quo. At the same time Moscow and Washington sought to curtail the incredibly expensive and dangerous arms race that had persisted in the 1950s and 1960s.

In some respects, the NPT has been the greatest achievement of the Brezhnev regime, as it continues to exist today. It has not always worked – some states have avoided ratifying the treaty and others have withdrawn - but even as the number of nuclear-armed states has increased since 1968, the NPT has more than likely impeded the potential development of a nuclear weapons free-for-all.

In 1968, Richard Nixon, a staunch anti-communist, was elected, but he would completely reshape American foreign policy by appointing strategic thinkers such as National Security Advisor Henry Kissinger. In fact, Nixon would signify a more wholehearted embrace of the concept of détente.

President Johnson had been desperate to withdraw troops from Vietnam, make some kind of accommodation with the communists, and even use the Soviets as an intermediary, but the Soviets were in no mood to make a deal with Johnson, particularly if they could contain the conflict to Southeast Asia. However, Nixon was much more of a challenge to Brezhnev – upon taking office, Nixon held himself out as an unpredictable leader who would potentially stop at nothing in securing American interests, even entertaining the use of nuclear weapons. As a hardliner, Nixon commanded respect in Moscow that Johnson did not enjoy.

As a means of bringing the Vietnamese communists (and by extension Brezhnev) to the negotiating table, Nixon actually escalated the conflict in Southeast Asia in 1969 and 1970. The American pesident increased the bombing of North Vietnam and then targeted the border areas utilized by communist guerrillas, most notoriously in Cambodia. With a sometimes bombastic inner circle of foreign policy hawks, the Nixon administration did indeed give the impression that they were willing to escalate the conflict and its growing brutality until it had achieved at least some of its objectives.

As an ally of Hanoi, this created further difficulties for the Soviets, who were also competing with the Chinese for ideological influence in North Vietnam. Both sides also had to deal with the emergence of the "Non-Aligned Movement" in the 1960s, a group of mainly recently independent countries that wanted to avoid alliances with the superpowers, or at least pursue a degree of autonomy within their foreign policy. As well as being suspicious of American and Chinese motives, Brezhnev also wanted to dampen the appeal of the Non-Aligned Movement, where the old Soviet nemesis Tito had become a leading light.

The Brezhnev regime was reactive in foreign policy terms during this era, unable to set the agenda on any major theme, and it would be the strategy of the Nixon administration that would alter Soviet policy in the 1970s, ushering in a period of significant détente. The Soviet leadership had the benefit of not needing to seek a democratic endorsement from their population, in sharp contrast with the United States.

With potentially decades in decision-making positions, it might have been expected that Moscow would be able to think strategically in the medium to long term, but the most influential strategic thinker of the period was Henry Kissinger. Born in Germany in the 1920s, Kissinger's family had fled the Nazis, emigrating to the United States in the 1930s. Kissinger was a student of realpolitik, very much in keeping with the German political tradition, and as an academic in the 1950s and 1960s, Kissinger had formed a complex, if at times somewhat sterile theory of the Cold War. Upon coming into office, the Nixon administration was faced with the urgent challenge of ending the Vietnam War. Kissinger believed he could do this while simultaneously reducing the overall tension in the Cold War and locking in America's rivals into a more sustainable international order. For this he would exploit what he perceived as the weakness of the Brezhnev regime: China. By the end of his time in office, he would exploit, if unwittingly, another pressure point: human rights. At the same time, the approach of Kissinger and Nixon greatly attracted the Soviets because it seemed to indicate the Americans had accepted the USSR as an equal partner in geopolitics.

In his own telling, Kissinger wanted to end the rigidity, as he saw it, in international politics.[1] The key was to undermine the Soviet support for North Vietnam, allow America to withdraw from Southeast Asia, and reduce the arms race. As mentioned previously, many in the West had not realized the tensions between the USSR and China as a result of the Sino-Soviet split, and the Nixon administration now sought to use this Achilles heel to wring concessions from Brezhnev. Kissinger opened a "back channel" to China via Pakistan, offering the prospect of talks. At the same time, the American table tennis team was surprisingly given permission to visit China for exhibition games against a Chinese team, becoming known as "Ping Pong Diplomacy." The trip, in the summer of 1971, was deemed a great success and was used to pave the way for a political visit, which Kissinger described as "rapprochement."

Up until this point most Western countries, under the guidance of the United States, refused to recognize Chairman Mao's People's Republic of China and instead recognized Taiwan as the representative of the Chinese people. Taiwan occupied China's seat in the United Nations, and relations between China and the West had deteriorated further during the 1960s as the Cultural Revolution escalated. Any political overtures from Washington towards China, therefore, would be seen as a major policy U-turn, but this is in fact what happened. First, Henry Kissinger traveled to China to meet the Chinese Premier Zhou Enlai, and then Nixon met with Mao in 1972, shocking the world. Furthermore, the two leaders agreed to end the estrangement between the two countries, shaking the Brezhnev regime to the core.

---

[1] CNN, *Cold War* (TV Series, produced by Jeremy Isaacs and Pat Mitchell, 1998)

Moscow now feared that it would be geopolitically boxed in from all sides by a hostile West and a rogue China from the East. The Brezhnev regime feared that an "anti-Soviet coalition" was being formed, although in hindsight the likelihood of anything like this occurring between China and America seemed remote.[2] Nevertheless, Kissinger and Nixon's so-called "triangulation" strategy worked according to plan, rapidly bringing the Soviets to the negotiation table as well and Vietnamese towards a settlement to end the war. The Americans suspected that if Moscow brought influence to bear over the North Vietnamese communists, they were more likely to make some actual concessions at the long-running Paris peace talks. Washington had been seeking a meeting with the Soviets for some time, and although Moscow agreed in principle, the Soviets had been consistently putting off the date of any summit, with the Americans seemingly stuck in a never-ending quagmire in Vietnam.

This all changed once Nixon and Kissinger played the so-called "China card."[3] Kissinger's direct line to the Kremlin went through Soviet ambassador to the United States in Washington, Anatoly Dobrynin who he met regularly. In this way the two superpowers could frame the negotiations that would take place at the summit which was quickly arranged after Nixon's visit to China.

President Nixon visited the Soviet Union on May 22, 1972, becoming the first American leader to visit the Kremlin. Moscow had a number of objectives regarding any agreement with the United States. The Soviets wanted a reduction in arms buildup, a restriction on nuclear weapons, and a tacit guarantee that the nuclear status quo would be maintained. The Soviets were concerned about defensive weapons such as anti-ballistic devices that could neutralize their arsenal. They also wanted the Americans to back them against China in their intra-communist disagreement. The U.S. never truly supported the Soviets over the Chinese, knowing that this lever could reap huge dividends, but the Americans did agree to arms limitation.

The Moscow summit was a success for both sides. Brezhnev and his allies took Nixon and Kissinger to his country *dacha* (home in the countryside) and, along with Kosygin and Podgorny, berated them for several hours over their actions in Southeast Asia before seamlessly moving to high-level diplomacy and agreeing to a number of the key principles of détente. Clearly, the Soviets were enthusiastic to limit offensive and defensive nuclear weapons.

The positive outcome of the Moscow talks played very well back on all sides. Nixon was received as a leader who had reduced the dangerous levels of tension in the Cold War, and for Brezhnev, détente created breathing space and some degree of stability in the Soviet Union and the wider communist world. China slowly drifted away from its revolutionary behavior, and relations between China and Russia gradually improved.

---

[2] CNN, *Cold War* (TV Series, produced by Jeremy Isaacs and Pat Mitchell, 1998)
[3] Godfrey Hodgson, *People's Century: From the dawn of the century to the eve of the millennium* (Godalming: BBC Books, 1998)

The most immediate impact of détente was on Southeast Asia. The Americans achieved their short-term goal by meeting the North Vietnamese more seriously at the negotiating table in Paris. The broad principles of a peace agreement were fleshed out during the rest of 1972. Hanoi, however, was reluctant to finalize the accords, which led to a wave of brutal bombings at the turn of the year by the Americans, the so-called "Christmas Bombings."[4] The callous, blunt instrument of aerial bombing served its purpose in American eyes. In January 1973, an agreement was reached between North Vietnam and South Vietnam, allowing the Americans to withdraw and satisfy public opinion at home. Tens of thousands of American troops and millions of Vietnamese had died in the conflict, and the agreement lasted just over two years until April 1975, when the communists overran the South Vietnamese army and forcibly unified the country. By this time, Nixon had been forced from office thanks to Watergate.

The most lasting impact of détente was nuclear arms limitation. Alongside the NPT, there would be two other major agreements signed between the superpowers. The Anti-Ballistic Missile Treaty (ABM Treaty) was signed by Nixon and Brezhnev at the Moscow summit, designed to limit defensive weapons that could neutralize either side's offensive missiles. Although counterintuitive in principle, the ABM Treaty was supposed to create a level playing field and ultimately deter either side from using nuclear weapons of any kind.

The Strategic Arms Limitation Talks (SALT) were a long-running series of negotiations that had begun during Nixon's first year in office in 1969 and based in the Finnish capital Helsinki. It culminated in the first SALT treaty, also signed in Moscow during Nixon's visit in May 1972. SALT sought to limit offensive nuclear weapons, intercontinental ballistic missiles (ICBMs), and other varieties of weapons launched from sea and land. It was a major step forward after two decades of nuclear weapons stockpiling.

The environment of détente also led to some degree of reconciliation between East and West Germany. Previously seen as one of the areas most likely to lead to a conflagration, West German Chancellor Willy Brandt, in power from 1969-1974, reversed the policy of his predecessors, which had been to ignore the East German state and refuse to deal with countries that recognized it. Brandt visited Poland and the Soviet Union, showing a remarkable level of contrition for the crimes of the Nazis and reaching agreements with the communist bloc. Most notably, Brandt met with East German leaders, and the two states agreed to reduce tension and improve relations, including family visits across the Berlin Wall.[5]

Known as *Ostpolitik* in German, this local détente both satisfied and worried Brezhnev's government. The policy appeared to recognize the post-war status quo, including the acceptance of a Soviet-led sphere of influence in Central and Eastern Europe. Conversely, *Ostpolitik* worried

---

[4] Rebecca Kesby, 'North Vietnam, 1972: The Christmas bombing of Hanoi', *BBC News*, 24 December 2012, https://www.bbc.com/news/magazine-20719382, [accessed 14 May 2019]

[5] Mary Fulbrook, *History of Germany, 1918-2000: the divided nation* (Oxford: Blackwell, 2002)

the superpowers because it suggested an independent foreign policy in Bonn and Berlin, as well as the possibility of a reunified Germany and revival of German nationalism. This would indeed come to pass, but not until the next phase of détente in the late 1980s, and when it did occur, both superpowers embraced German reunification.

Brezhnev visited the American president in June 1973 and expressed utter bemusement at Nixon's domestic troubles around the Watergate saga.[6] In the authoritarian Soviet Union, scandals never entered the minds of the country's leaders. Although without the kind of treaty signing that had occurred the previous year in Moscow, Brezhnev and Nixon vowed to work together to further peace between the two superpowers. A little over a year later, Nixon was forced to resign, but the détente process continued for several more years.

**Brezhnev and Nixon meeting in 1973**

The culmination of the détente process was the 1975 Helsinki Final Act, signed by every European state and both superpowers.[7] It had been set in motion by the developments of the previous years, the SALT discussions, and the high-level summits American and Soviet officials. Brezhnev himself addressed the 1975 Helsinki conference, highlighting the need for world peace

---

[6] Robert Coalson, 'A Surprisingly Candid Chat Between Nixon and Brezhnev', *The Atlantic*, 26 August 2013, https://www.theatlantic.com/international/archive/2013/08/a-surprisingly-candid-chat-between-nixon-and-brezhnev/278981/, [accessed 14 May 2019]

[7] Gerald Knaus, "Europe and Azerbaijan: The End of Shame," *Journal of Democracy,* (2015, pp. 5-18)

through a new accommodation between East and West. Brezhnev, although by now ailing somewhat, wanted to present himself as a statesman and peacemaker. Indeed, since he came to power in 1964, his regime had overseen a better standard of living for the Soviet people and managed to avoid, by and large, the conflicts of his Western counterparts.

Ironically, with the benefit of hindsight, many historians have subsequently cited Brezhnev's signing of the Helsinki accords as the communist bloc's death sentence, lighting the fuse of a time bomb under his own country's existence. How did Brezhnev turn this apparent victory into a road to defeat for the Soviet Union and its system of alliances?

The Soviets were eager to conclude the Helsinki talks, which had actually started earlier in the 1970s, because they would effectively recognize the post-1945 borders in Europe. This held particular attraction for the Soviet Politburo because it appeared to accept the separation of Europe into American and Soviet spheres of influence. What is worth keeping in mind here is that for much of the period after the start of the Cold War, Moscow believed that the West was working to undermine its influence in Central and Eastern Europe, encouraging the revolts of 1953, 1956 and 1968, all while recognizing the communist regime in East Germany.[8] Helsinki would solve all these difficulties in one overarching agreement. Yet, the devil was in the detail. While the first two articles, or baskets, of the accords concentrated on hard power issues, the Third Basket focused on humanitarian themes, including the recognition of liberal values such as human rights. Pursued by the West Germans, the Third Basket was initially vehemently opposed by Moscow and also resisted by Secretary of State Henry Kissinger for the same reason: both Kissinger and his Soviet counterparts believed that the human rights provisions would introduce a degree of instability into the situation in Europe. That belief proved prescient.

Despite their respective doubts, the Soviets, Americans, and every communist regime signed the Helsinki Final Act on August 1, 1975.[9] Included within this third article was provision for a new organization, the Commission on Security and Cooperation in Europe (the CSCE), which would monitor both security and the values set out in the accord. By all accounts, it was long-term Politburo member and veteran communist Andrei Gromyko who convinced his colleagues to approve the agreement by outlining the importance of the border issues and recognition of the status quo. Gromyko believed that Moscow could override any concerns about human rights with the simple invocation of sovereignty.[10] The West had shown it was not prepared to intervene in internal communist disputes in Europe, such as in Czechoslovakia in 1968, so any commitment to values like human rights would be hollow.

This turned out to be a fatal misreading of the situation. The communists did not allow for the possibility that the populations in the communist world might take these provisions seriously, but

---

[8] Mary Fulbrook, *History of Germany, 1918-2000: the divided nation* (Oxford: Blackwell, 2002)
[9] OSCE, Helsinki Final Act, 1 August 1975, https://www.osce.org/helsinki-final-act, [accessed 14 May 2019]
[10] CNN, *Cold War* (TV Series, produced by Jeremy Isaacs and Pat Mitchell, 1998)

shortly after the signing of the Helsinki Final Act, dissident groups cited them in their underground activities in Czechoslovakia.[11] Within the space of a few years, the language of human rights would be used from within to undermine authoritarian regimes across the communist world.

By the late 1970s, Brezhnev was in poor health.[12] A heavy smoker and drinker, Brezhnev had by all accounts increased his alcohol intake in the 1970s and simultaneously began to suffer a series of serious medical issues, most notably heart and respiratory problems. He suffered his first heart attack in 1975 and also experienced strokes.

What is perhaps most surprising was that he was allowed to continue as leader while having such serious health difficulties. It has been suggested that the Soviet leadership was concerned that Brezhnev's resignation would stimulate a power struggle and even social unrest. Most transfers of power within the Soviet system had led to some degree of social upheaval, either within the USSR or in its satellite states, or both.

This begs the question of who was making the decisions at the top of the Party in the late 1970s and early 1980s. It seems that a consensus was often found in a Politburo packed with long-term Soviet communists who viewed the world in similar ways, such as Yuri Andropov, Mikhail Suslov, Andrei Gromyko, and Dmitry Ustinov. Historians such as Vladislav Zubok have posited that these Soviet leaders viewed détente a consequence of Soviet military strength, allowing the superpower to flex its military muscles.[13]

However it happened, one of the regime's most fateful decisions was the invasion of Afghanistan, which started on December 26, 1979 when most Western officials were on their Christmas breaks. Afghanistan had long been the scourge of much larger powers attempting to dominate the territory, continuing up until the present day. During the Cold War, the country bordered the Soviet Union republics of Uzbekistan, Tajikistan and Turkmenistan, and Moscow therefore came to believe that securing a communist regime in this border country was in its vital national interests. In April 1978, a communist revolution occurred in Afghanistan, an extremely poor state, bringing to power Nur Muhammad Taraki. This was met with resistance from religious conservatives and an early version of the Islamic mujahideen fighters. The situation was chaotic and highly unstable, and there were threats of coups and countercoups while Taraki and his Foreign Minister Hafizullah Amin committed tens of thousands of murders as the regime attempted to consolidate power. In September 1979, Amin himself overthrew Taraki and had him arrested and murdered.

---

[11] Emily Tamkin, "In Charter 77, Czech Dissidents Charted New Territory," *Foreign Policy*, 3 February 2017, https://foreignpolicy.com/2017/02/03/in-charter-77-czech-dissidents-charted-new-territory/, [accessed 10 April 2019]

[12] William J. Tompson, *The Soviet Union under Brezhnev*, (Routledge, 2014), p. 180.

[13] Vladislav M. Zubok, *Failed Empire: The Soviet Union in the Cold War from Stalin to Gorbachev* (The University of North Carolina Press, 2007), p.259.

Brezhnev was concerned about the chain of events in the country and had not supported Amin's coup. With the country descending into anarchy, the Soviets intervened to remove Amin, who they replaced with Babrak Karmal, and sent in a small force to pacify the anti-government agitation, securing a communist Afghanistan. There is some evidence to suggest that Brezhnev himself was opposed to the invasion and was still attached to the idea of détente.[14] Indeed, the two superpowers were due to sign another SALT agreement, but this was ultimately never ratified by Congress, which grew hostile over any further rapprochement with untrustworthy adversaries.

If Brezhnev initially opposed the intervention, he was apparently persuaded by his more hawkish colleagues, namely Andropov, Suslov, and Ustinov,[15] who suggested if the USSR "lost" Afghanistan, the Americans could use it in the same way they exploited Cuba for strategic reasons.[16] NATO's decision at the same time to deploy new Pershing missiles in West Germany may have also hardened attitudes in Moscow.[17]

When Soviet tanks rolled into Afghanistan on December 26, 1979, it caused outrage across the Western world, but the Red Army's "short" intervention would last almost 10 years and lead to the deaths of almost 15,000 Soviet soldiers, tens of thousands of Afghan fighters, and maybe up to two million Afghan civilians. It proved to be just as unwinnable as America's calamitous intervention in Vietnam.[18]

As the Brezhnev regime became increasingly sucked into the Afghan theater, the Carter administration, which was focused on human rights and the ethical dimensions of the Cold War, was replaced by the ardent anti-communist Reagan administration. Along with Britain's Margaret Thatcher, Reagan was an aggressive critic of the USSR's actions, and he extended Carter's ideological criticism of the communist system, famously describing the Soviet Union as an "Evil Empire" shortly after Brezhnev's death.[19]

---

[14] Vladislav M. Zubok, *Failed Empire: The Soviet Union in the Cold War from Stalin to Gorbachev* (The University of North Carolina Press, 2007), p.261.
[15] William J. Tompson, *The Soviet Union under Brezhnev*, (Routledge, 2014), p. 29.
[16] Vladislav M. Zubok, *Failed Empire: The Soviet Union in the Cold War from Stalin to Gorbachev* (The University of North Carolina Press, 2007), p.263.
[17] Vladislav M. Zubok, *Failed Empire: The Soviet Union in the Cold War from Stalin to Gorbachev* (The University of North Carolina Press, 2007), p.253.
[18] William J. Tompson, *The Soviet Union under Brezhnev*, (Routledge, 2014), p. 112.
[19] Godfrey Hodgson, *People's Century: From the dawn of the century to the eve of the millennium* (Godalming: BBC Books, 1998)

**Thatcher**

Whereas earlier in his tenure, Brezhnev could make some claim to the moral high ground, by the early 1980s his regime was under siege by critics attempting to undermine his country's ideological foundations. Matters were not helped by Brezhnev's poor health, which deteriorated further in 1981 and allowed a collection of hardliners to make key decisions. Andropov, Suslov, Gromyko, and Ustinov further damaged Moscow's international prestige.

During Brezhnev's final years, the economy continued to slump. In terms of GDP, the Soviet economy continued to grow, but the expansion of 1-2% was far too low for a developing country such as the USSR. The Soviets would spend much of the 1980s attempting to reduce spending and increase economic output, but Brezhnev and his advisors were wholly unqualified to accomplish that, and they repeatedly failed to significantly improve living conditions.

Although the Soviet Union had done its best to insulate it from the global capitalist economy, in the early 1980s this was becoming difficult. Interest rates had been hiked by the U.S. Federal Reserve in an attempt to squeeze inflation out of its own economy, and with falling commodity prices, these trends damaged a number of governments, in particular communist allies of the Soviet Union. The situation would grow even more desperate as the decade progressed, and even as the Soviet economy remained sclerotic, the Politburo was overly reluctant to implement reforms.

Brezhnev and his colleagues were also resistant to any criticism regarding human rights. It continued to impede the emigration of Soviet Jews and fill jails with political prisoners. Rather than the Stalin-era network of Gulag prisons, separate towns were established to keep and seal off troublesome citizens, such as "PERM-36," to the North East of Moscow.[20] It was in this kind of setting that Andrei Sakharov continued to be held until his release in 1986. Sakharov was famous across the world, and his persistent hunger strikes threatened to further embarrass the Soviet regime.

Brezhnev did not wield power in 1982 despite remaining in office. He rarely appeared in public and had another serious stroke that May. By the time he died on November 10, 1982, other members of the Politburo had been vying for the top position as it became clear that Brezhnev was close to death.

**Gorbachev's Immediate Challenges**

Mikhail Suslov, who was already 79 himself, had been assumed to be one of the favorites, but he died in January 1982, paving the way for Yuri Andropov. As the former head of the KGB, Andropov was obviously connected with the levers of power within the Soviet Union, so it was perhaps unsurprising that he assumed power in a relatively straightforward fashion shortly after Brezhnev's death. To the outside world, Andropov looked like he would pursue a tougher line than Brezhnev, but in reality he had already been crucial in making decisions the past few years, so there was plenty of continuity.

---

[20] BBC Radio 4, 'I was imprisoned in Stalin's Gulag', *Witness*, 9 September 2015, https://www.bbc.com/news/av/magazine-34155914/i-was-imprisoned-in-stalin-s-gulag, [accessed 4 December 2018]

**Andropov**

Andropov was 68 when he took office, and while that was relatively young for a member of the Soviet Politburo, he died on February 9, 1984 of kidney failure. He was replaced by an even older man, Konstantin Chernenko, who was 72 and ill when he came to power. He died as a result of respiratory, heart, and liver problems on March 10, 1985. Mikhail Gorbachev took power in the Soviet Union a day later, at the age of 54.

**Gorbachev**

As with most communist leaders during the era, little was known about the individual preferences of each member of the Politburo. From the outside, Gorbachev appeared to be an orthodox communist likely to continue the policies of his predecessor. Born in 1931 in the Stavropol Krai region of Russia, located in the North Caucasus, Gorbachev had been a dutiful communist. Rising through the ranks of the regional party, he became head of the Stavropol region in 1970 and a member of the key Central Committee of the Soviet Union the following year. This marked Gorbachev's entry onto the national stage, and in 1980, he became a full member of the inner circle, the Politburo. Intriguingly,

Gorbachev's closest ally on the Politburo was Yuri Andropov, the former head of the KGB and seemingly hard-line, orthodox communist. It may be a sign of Gorbachev's political cunning that he garnered Andropov's support, or simply that he exhibited few signs of the reforming zeal that would so mark him out as different to his colleagues after he became party General Secretary in 1985.

Indeed, Gorbachev was Andropov's favored successor, as the aging leader considered the younger man capable of breaking out of the cycle of geriatric leaders that characterized this period of Soviet politics. When Andropov died in 1984, however, the compromise candidate was the frail Konstantin Chernenko, who was actually older than Andropov. It would not be until Chernenko's death that Gorbachev actually took power.

Perhaps the only exception to the belief that Gorbachev showed no pedigree of reform came in 1984 when he met British Prime Minister Margaret Thatcher. The meeting was judged subsequently to be a sign that if Gorbachev became a future Soviet leader, the relationship between the West and the communist world could potentially improve markedly. Thatcher had been described by the Soviet leadership as an "Iron Lady" before she became Prime Minister, a sobriquet she liked so much she encouraged its use, and by 1984 she had established herself as a foreign policy hawk, particularly after the 1982 Falklands War. Nevertheless, Thatcher had been infuriated by the Soviet leadership, mostly due their stilted and unimaginative manner, and inflexibility regarding policy.

In December 1984, just months before he was given the opportunity to lead the Soviet Union, Mikhail Gorbachev visited Thatcher in Britain. He was invited to the Prime Minister's countryside retreat, *Chequers*, for wide-ranging discussions on foreign policy, nuclear weapons, the geopolitical situation in Eastern Europe, and more.[21] Thatcher was surprized by Gorbachev's openness and immediately recognized that he was a different kind of Soviet leader,[22] famously declaring, "I like Mr Gorbachev. We can do business together." The timing of the meeting was serendipitous for the Gorbachev-Thatcher relationship. The next time they met was at the funeral of Konstantin Chernenko in March 1985 as Gorbachev prepared to take power.[23]

What had been clear to Thatcher in 1984 was that Gorbachev was animated about the Strategic Defense Initiative (SDI) and seemed ready to pre-negotiate other arms limitation talks, including offensive weapons, in return for concessions on SDI.[24] The project was widely derided and jokingly referred to as "Star Wars," costing hundreds of billions and never getting anywhere near implementation. In terms of Cold War strategy, however, SDI worked perfectly, and the Soviets took the threat of SDI at face value. If Star Wars became operational, it would render the Soviet nuclear arsenal redundant against the United States. Western Europe would then be the Soviets' target, which is why SDI concerned both the Soviet bloc and American allies in Europe, especially Thatcher. In terms of treaty obligations, SDI also effectively breached the terms of the ABM (Anti-Ballistic Missile) agreement, made between the US and Soviets in 1968. The idea of ABM was to set a level playing field and curb the arms race.

---

[21] John Campbell, *Margaret Thatcher Volume Two: The Iron Lady* (Random House, 2003), pp. 285-286.
[22] Margaret Thatcher, *The Downing Street Years* (Harper Collins, 1993), pp. 459-463.
[23] John Campbell, *Margaret Thatcher Volume Two: The Iron Lady* (Random House, 2003), p. 286.
[24] Charles Moore, *Margaret Thatcher The Authorized Biography: Volume Two Everything She Wants* (Allen Lane, 2015), pp. 232-233.

In December 1984, neither Thatcher nor Gorbachev were in positions to negotiate with each other, but nevertheless the message was relayed to the Reagan administration that Gorbachev would be a useful contact for better relations between the West and Moscow. Little did they know that they would get the chance to deal with Gorbachev, this time in a position of ultimate responsibility, much quicker than anticipated.

Despite the signs of an opening between Gorbachev and Britain, the situation he inherited in March 1985 was challenging to say the least. The Soviets had escalated the Cold War in the late 1970s by stepping up its support for left wing movements and governments in Africa and Central America, and the Americans had elected the anti-communist Ronald Reagan in November 1980. It wasn't long before President Reagan called the Soviet Union an "evil empire," and he would famously demand that Gorbachev tear down the Berlin Wall.

# Reagan and Gorbachev in 1986

With positions toughening on both sides, superpower tension increased in the early 1980s, and the arms race seemed to be back after a period of détente in the early 1970s. It was during this period that an escalation of the Cold War seemed possible, either by design or through a miscalculation. An example of the former was the deployment of the new Pershing nuclear weapons by NATO into West Germany despite vigorous dissent among Western domestic populations. In 1983, a NATO exercise, Operation Able Archer, triggered panic on the Soviet side and came alarmingly close to a nuclear escalation. Moreover, the Soviets shot down a civilian plane, South Korean Air flight KAL007, in August 1983 which led to increased hostility, threats, and counterthreats on both sides.

The United States hosted the 1984 Olympic Games in Los Angeles, and the event was boycotted by the Soviets in retaliation for the American boycott of the 1980 games in Moscow. The West constantly criticized the Soviet war in Afghanistan and offered material support to the anti-Soviet Islamic militias known as the Mujahideen. The Soviets meanwhile lambasted the Reagan administration for its wholehearted support of right-wing forces in Latin America, many of which committed grave human rights violations, such as in El Salvador and Nicaragua.

The Soviet regime that Gorbachev inherited believed that Star Wars would give the United States overwhelming military superiority, and many of Gorbachev's subsequent decisions were based upon the premise that the Soviet Union needed to make an accommodation with the US on nuclear weapons or reestablish the principles of the ABM and other arms limitation agreements, such as SALT (Strategic Arms Limitation Talks). What made this even more urgent was that Gorbachev clearly understood that the USSR could not afford to match the US on arms, even in the unlikely event that it could develop technology like SDI. The true strength of the Soviets during the Cold War was in the intelligence sphere, but this was unlikely to provide the resources to match such an undertaking as SDI. Indeed, part of Gorbachev's strategy was to reduce the spending commitments that the Soviets had built up during the Cold War.

Furthermore, Gorbachev was also faced with the war in Afghanistan. Having invaded the country at the end of 1979 as a means of propping up a communist regime in Kabul, the Soviet army and air force had become bogged down in guerrilla warfare. There was little attachment from the Afghan population towards communism, and the main opposition formed around religious groups and militias. These mujahideen were increasingly supported by US hardware, most infamously surface to air missiles, so-called "stingers" which began to terrorize Soviet planes and helicopters. Gorbachev had always been skeptical of the war despite the fact Andropov was one of its architects. With the Soviets in an Afghan quagmire by 1985, Gorbachev would also quickly seek to extricate his country from the conflict.

## Gorbachev's Tentative Domestic Reforms

Gorbachev came to power as a slow economic and political crisis gripped the Soviet Union, though this was not immediately obvious to outside observers. After all, the communist system intended to iron out the boom and bust tendencies of a market economy, and provide consistent, centrally-planned growth and increasing living standards. However, bubbling under the surface were serious problems, and Gorbachev moved quickly to denounce the approach of his predecessors - who were conveniently no longer alive - as flawed. In particular he vilified the Brezhnev era as one of corruption and stagnation, and indeed, the Soviet economy had become sclerotic by the mid-1980s, devoid of momentum, dynamism and new ideas.[25]

What made things particularly acute was that the United States had managed to apply enough pressure on oil-producing countries like Saudi Arabia for the oil price to fall. Oil prices had been particularly damaging to the West during the 1970s as the OPEC cartel increased prices following the 1973 Arab-Israeli War, then the 1979 Iranian Revolution. In the 1980s, lower prices had the opposite effect, starving the oil-producing USSR of vital hard currency. The limited economic data available on the Soviet Union showed how its economy slowed in the late 1970s, and did not recover for the rest of its existence.[26] In addition, although industrialized, the Soviet Union still had the hallmarks of a developing economy and therefore required much higher rates of growth to improve its population's standard of living. This was the economic situation that Gorbachev inherited in March 1985.

Gorbachev was a more imaginative leader than his predecessors. Whereas most other Soviet leaders would have been guided by events, particularly in the economic sphere, Gorbachev had already worked out his own theory of his country's ailments. To summarize, his analysis shared much with the "Prague Spring" of late 1960s Czechoslovakia, where communist leader Alexander Dubček had outlined a reform project known as "socialism with a human face." Gorbachev's version of these principles drew on similar themes: socialism in and of itself was a virtuous system, but it needed improving. The way to do this was to unleash the energy of its citizens by loosening political constraints. Therefore, Gorbachev sought to reduce the omnipotent fear of dissent in the mid-1980s and unleash a wave of creative power that would drive the country's economy and increase growth, living standards, and the USSR's position relative to the United States. The new Soviet leader still believed that Soviet communism was a superior system to Western liberal capitalism, and that it simply needed reform.[27]

The sequencing of his programme was crucial. Political liberalization would come first, which would lead to economic results. It was the polar opposite to what was already underway in Deng Xiaoping's communist China. which focused on economic liberalization while maintaining

---

[25] Mark Gilbert, *Cold War Europe: The Politics of a Contested Continent* (Rowman & Littlefield, 2014), p. 142.
[26] Edwin Bacon & Mark Sandle, *Brezhnev Reconsidered* (Palgrave Macmillan, 2002), p. 40.
[27] CNN, *Cold War* (TV Series, produced by Jeremy Isaacs and Pat Mitchell, 1998)

political strictures.

In his first months in office, Gorbachev showed glimpses of the road he wanted to take. He traveled around the USSR, often stopping to speak to ordinary people on the street, encouraging them to speak their minds. The Soviet leader also discouraged portraits of him, hoping to avoid the kind of cult of personality of previous leaders that Gorbachev believed to be inane. He also packed the Politburo with reformers and supporters, knowing that the changes he planned to enact would likely lead to resistance from orthodox hardliners. He made the veteran foreign minister Andrei Gromyko head of state, replaced him with reformer Eduard Shevardnadze, and brought key allies Alexander Yakovlev and Anatoly Lukyanov into the Politburo.

**Yakovlev**

**Shevardnadze**

Gorbachev's first big idea in domestic affairs was *Perestroika,* or restructuring, and targeted work practices and economic policy. The Soviet leader had identified the inefficient approach to production as a key impediment to better economic performance. Gorbachev was desperate to find a way to improve the productivity of the Soviet economy, without actually transforming it into a market system. His Perestroika programme intended to improve the communist system. At its core, however, Perestroika was vague and nebulous. As historian Vladislav Zubok has noted, Perestroika "eluded definition and systemization."[28] The forces it set free, along with later political liberalising, set the country on a path to tumult, including within the Politburo.[29] The

---

[28] Vladislav M. Zubok, *Failed Empire: The Soviet Union in the Cold War from Stalin to Gorbachev* (The University of North Carolina Press, 2007), p. 279.
[29] Michael McFaul, *Russia's Unfinished Revolution: Political Change from Gorbachev to Putin* (Cornell University Press, 2002), p. 78.

obstacles to economic reform were huge.[30] With towns and cities effectively monopsonies, that is to say there was often one major employer or factory, there was no competition and few incentives for Soviets to increase productivity. Although in the past communist regimes had set ludicrous production targets, these were treated with great scepticism, if not derision, by the 1980s. Without private property, central planners also found it hard to encourage greater efficiency or generate energy around reform.

Gorbachev launched his Perestroika agenda in a speech in May 1985 and, unusually for a communist leader, took the opportunity to criticize the regime's economic policies. That said, there was little concrete action for the first two years of Perestroika, save for encouragement from the top to improve efficiency and productivity. The Gorbachev regime thought, erroneously, that removing inefficient and corrupt bureaucrats may suffice to encourage better economic performance, marking a cautious start to "modernization."[31]

More substantial changes came after the 27th Congress of the Soviet Communist Party in 1987, but Gorbachev's failure to fundamentally revive the Soviet economy was one of the crucial reasons he oversaw the eventual collapse of the USSR. A related factor was political reform, which gave Soviet citizens the opportunity to air their pent-up grievances, as well as provide oxygen to ideas antithetical to the Soviet model, such as nationalism. Gorbachev, however, appeared to have much greater success with this programme in his first two years in office, the name of which became recognizable around the world: *Glasnost*. Meaning "openness and transparency," Gorbachev adopted the term as a slogan in June 1986. Glasnost was a relaxation of censorship, even encouraging - at least by Soviet standards - freedom of expression. This was initially focused on art and literature and gave unprecedented freedom to publishers.[32]

Gorbachev delegated the programme to his ally, Alexander Yakovlev, who set in motion a series of astonishingly liberal measures.[33] Yakovlev encouraged the setting up of reformist publications and then installed liberal editors. These titles, such as *Moscow News* and *Ogonek* discussed previously unheard-of taboos in the cultural, economic and political spheres. Suddenly Soviet history was open to discussion and debate. After almost 70 years of suffocating political repression, Glasnost was like a breath of fresh air, one that many Soviet citizens were unprepared for. Gorbachev passed laws in 1987 that provided further freedom of expression and association.[34] In 1987 Moscow stopped blocking the signals of Western radio stations such as Germany's *Deutsche Welle*, the US's *Voice of America* and Britain's *BBC*.[35] After Perestroika, the Glasnost

---

[30] Archie Brown, *The Gorbachev Factor* (Oxford University Press, 1996), p. 136.
[31] Vladislav M. Zubok, *Failed Empire: The Soviet Union in the Cold War from Stalin to Gorbachev* (The University of North Carolina Press, 2007), p. 279.
[32] Michael McFaul, *Russia's Unfinished Revolution: Political Change from Gorbachev to Putin* (Cornell University Press, 2002), p. 64.
[33] Michael McFaul, *Russia's Unfinished Revolution: Political Change from Gorbachev to Putin* (Cornell University Press, 2002), p. 64.
[34] Michael McFaul, *Russia's Unfinished Revolution: Political Change from Gorbachev to Putin* (Cornell University Press, 2002), p. 64.

liberalisation agenda garnered further enemies in the Soviet corridors of power.

A well-known early beneficiary of Gorbachev's new agenda was Andrei Sakharov. One of the communist world's most famous political prisoners, Sakharov was a Soviet nuclear scientist who had begun criticizing the regime in the 1960s, invoking human rights over the following decade. A thorn in the side of the Brezhnev government, Sakharov was jailed after his participation in protests against the invasion of Afghanistan in 1979. Isolated in Gorky, Sakharov had engaged in hunger strikes and was an intermittent embarrassment for the Soviet regime, which was terrified that he would die in jail. One of Sakharov's principle complaints was that the Soviet Union had signed up to the 1975 Helsinki Final Act without implementing any of the treaty's human rights provisions. Gorbachev himself would take these commitments far more seriously and essentially closed the residual elements of the Gulag prison network which had so tainted the reputation of the USSR over the course of its history. In fact, Gorbachev would stay relatively close to Sakharov after his release as the human rights activist took full advantage of Glasnost to pursue a position of unofficial political leadership before becoming a Deputy in the USSR's first ever elections in 1989.

---

[35] Vladislav M. Zubok, *Failed Empire: The Soviet Union in the Cold War from Stalin to Gorbachev* (The University of North Carolina Press, 2007), p. 298.

## Sakharov

One of the rapid byproducts of the Glasnost agenda was a desire by some for more democratic accountability in the USSR. As Michael McFaul has outlined, this allowed Sakharov to become the "moral leader of Russia's emerging democratic opposition."[36] During this heady period, many of Gorbachev's inner circle believed they could ride the tiger of liberalization while continuing the centrally-controlled communist system. The essential contradiction within this point of view would only become obvious later.

Two of the men who turned Gorbachev's agenda into reality were both named Yakovlev, though they were unrelated. Alexander Yakovlev can be thought of as the "chief ideologist" of Perestroika.[37] Technically in charge of propaganda, Alexander Yakovlev effectively turned the Soviet Union into a more normal state, eliminating many of the false statements of past years. Promoted to the Politburo in 1987, he admitted to the Soviet Union's participation in the 1939 Molotov-Ribbentrop Pact, the agreement between Stalin and Hitler that had initially kept the USSR out of the Second World War. This was a highly unusual, but symbolic gesture for a Soviet politician. It also attracted the ire of the hardliners, who made it a priority to oust him, which they duly did after an attack on him at the 28th Congress in July 1990.

Meanwhile, Yegor Yakovlev was responsible for transforming the press environment of the USSR as editor and champion of a more open media setting. Yegor cultivated that most un-Soviet of things, a respected media outlet, with his work on *Moscow News*. Despite not being related, the two Yakovlev's were close and were key to the change in tone in Gorbachev's USSR.[38] Between the pair, amongst others, they helped bring the concept of objective truth closer to the Soviet people, but, as Arkady Ostrovsky has noted, without the official lies of Soviet propaganda, the state lacked legitimacy in many people's eyes.[39]

One of Gorbachev's earliest initiatives was his "war on alcoholism."[40] Launched at the same time as Perestroika in May 1985, most of the Politburo now adopted a curious stance.[41] Soviet leaders had been known for their penchant for drinking alcohol and would continue to be in the future, and Soviet leaders had long tolerated heavy drinking among the wider population as a means of distraction from the often-stultifying conditions of everyday life. This would all change under Gorbachev, who saw chronic alcoholism as another symptom of the malaise of Soviet

---

[36] Michael McFaul, *Russia's Unfinished Revolution: Political Change from Gorbachev to Putin* (Cornell University Press, 2002), p. 65.
[37] Arkady Ostrovsky, *The Invention of Russia: The Journey from Gorbachev's Freedom to Putin's War* (Atlantic Books, 2015), p. 13.
[38] Arkady Ostrovsky, *The Invention of Russia: The Journey from Gorbachev's Freedom to Putin's War* (Atlantic Books, 2015), p. 15.
[39] Arkady Ostrovsky, *The Invention of Russia: The Journey from Gorbachev's Freedom to Putin's War* (Atlantic Books, 2015), p. 15.
[40] Vladislav M. Zubok, *Failed Empire: The Soviet Union in the Cold War from Stalin to Gorbachev* (The University of North Carolina Press, 2007), p. 280.
[41] Archie Brown, *The Gorbachev Factor* (Oxford University Press, 1996), p. 141.

society, namely its poor productivity and general low morale. The anti-alcohol campaign, led by Yegor Ligachev, contained a number of strands, including general anti-alcohol propaganda and specified restrictions in the sale, supply, and distribution of alcohol. The campaign initially gained traction in part because Gorbachev was a light drinker in comparison with his peers. The restrictions on alcohol, however, became increasingly unpopular as the campaign wore on.

One of the most notorious events of the Gorbachev era was the nuclear disaster at the Chernobyl plant in April 1986. Despite his reputation for transparency, Gorbachev's woeful response to the catastrophe demonstrated the limits of his personal influence and capabilities in the USSR at this time. The longer-term problems would only become clear in the years ahead, but in 1986, the Soviet authorities attempted to keep news of the disaster a secret. It was only days after the explosion at the nuclear power plant that the regime admitted something had happened, and this was only after a nuclear power plant in Sweden had detected high levels of radiation. The lackluster response of the Soviet government ensured it was lambasted for incompetence across the world, and it heightened concerns over nuclear power in general, particularly in secretive and deceitful states such as the Soviet Union. Chernobyl is sure to be one of the most enduring aspects of Gorbachev's legacy, as the area is estimated to remain contaminated for decades, if not centuries.[42]

---

[42] Richard Pérez-Peña, "Decades Later and Far Away, Chernobyl Disaster Still Contaminates Milk," *The New York Times*, 8 June 2018, https://www.nytimes.com/2018/06/08/world/europe/chernobyl-nuclear-disaster-radiation-milk.html, [accessed 21 May 2019]

**A picture of the damage at Chernobyl after the accident**

## Gorbachev's Early Foreign Policy

In the mid-1980s, the communist world was in a state of flux. Many of the regimes in the region were wobbling.[43] Poland had only recently ended martial law, and in East Germany the regime was struggling for hard currency. Romania was under the full grip of its megalomaniac leader Nicolae Ceaușescu, who lived in splendor while subjecting his people to misery, living through freezing cold in the winter with little food or consumer goods on the shelves of shops. Hungary was one of the only countries to implement liberalizing economic reform, but Central and Eastern Europe were expected to toe Moscow's line. Whereas previously this might have involved a crackdown on reformists or dissidents, after Gorbachev came to power, the satellite

---

[43] CNN, *Cold War* (TV Series, produced by Jeremy Isaacs and Pat Mitchell, 1998)

states in Europe were now expected to pursue Glasnost and Perestroika. In some respects, Gorbachev actually expected communist leaders in Central and Eastern Europe to think for themselves, which proved to be a tough task. T

he other countries broadly aligned with the Soviet Union also struggled to keep up with Gorbachev's reforms, and nowhere was this as relevant as in communist Yugoslavia. After Tito's death in 1980, Yugoslavia appeared, for all intents and purposes, to be prospering, implementing its more flexible form of communism. Nevertheless, a more open political atmosphere posed serious problems for Belgrade, because if citizens could discuss politics in a more open environment, they could potentially discuss previously forbidden topics such as nationalism. This would prove as fatal for the Soviet Union as it proved later for Yugoslavia, but these issues were largely hidden from view in the first few years of the Gorbachev era.

Despite the increasingly belligerent rhetoric of the early 1980s, the Politburo wanted to return to détente.[44] In geopolitics, it is often easier for hardliners to make agreements with apparently sworn enemies. Reagan presented a much tougher foreign policy to the world, rhetorically lambasting the entire communist system and philosophy, offering material support for anti-communist forces in Central America, and deploying nuclear weapons in Western Europe to oppose the Soviet missiles there. He was a consistent critic of the Soviet involvement in Afghanistan and encouraged the CIA to provide aid to the anti-Soviet militias in that theatre. In short, Moscow saw Reagan as a potentially dangerous opponent who had raised the stakes in the Cold War, so Gorbachev's administration wanted to reduce Cold War tension and return to 1970s-style détente.

Ultimately, Reagan and Gorbachev developed a dialogue, assisted by intermediaries such as Thatcher and Canadian Prime Minister Pierre Trudeau, and they subsequently met at a serious of superpower summits. The SDI was the issue that urgently brought Gorbachev to the negotiating table. Foreign policy was tightly controlled by Gorbachev and his foreign minister, Eduard Shevardnadze, who had no previous experience in foreign affairs but did enjoy the confidence of the General Secretary.[45] Gorbachev and Shevardnadze pressed the Americans for a face-to-face meeting, seeking a commitment to reduce the number of offensive weapons and persuade Reagan to shelve the Star Wars project. Essentially, Gorbachev wanted a reversion to a 1972 version of détente in which both offensive and defensive weapons would be controlled and limited.

As it turned out, Reagan was actually a proponent of nuclear disarmament, a fact that only became clear as his second term progressed. The American president was actually open to any Soviet overture that involved reducing or removing the threat of nuclear weapons. Deterrence

---

[44] Vladislav M. Zubok, *Failed Empire: The Soviet Union in the Cold War from Stalin to Gorbachev* (The University of North Carolina Press, 2007), p. 280.
[45] Vladislav M. Zubok, *Failed Empire: The Soviet Union in the Cold War from Stalin to Gorbachev* (The University of North Carolina Press, 2007), p. 280.

had been the principle that had led to the arms race and then détente in the Cold War, yet Reagan thought deterrence was wrongheaded.[46] It would bring Reagan into a fierce dispute with other Western leaders such as Thatcher, as well as the hardliners in his own administration. Nevertheless, it was Thatcher who broke the logjam for a Reagan-Gorbachev meeting. By publicly endorsing Gorbachev and claiming he was someone with whom she could "do business," she had paved the way for a meeting with Reagan.

The first meeting between Reagan and Gorbachev came on November 19-20, 1985 in Geneva, but the signs had not been promising leading up to the summit. The Americans dismissed out of hand any concessions over Star Wars, and a reduction in offensive warheads also seemed out of reach. The meeting, however, yielded some results insofar as the two leaders showed some warmth towards each other. Meeting in private there appeared little common ground and few points of agreement between the pair, but they were both optimistic politicians and developed a rapport. At the time, Reagan's aides and some of the Western press were concerned that the American would be bamboozled by the younger, perhaps wily Soviet leader, and indeed, despite the personal bond, Gorbachev was dismissive of Reagan's political views, famously telling his colleagues he considered the president a "troglodyte."[47]

Although a dialogue had opened between Reagan and Gorbachev, which was more than could be said for the previous six years, the two leaders left Geneva without any firm agreement or statement of aims. In and of itself, the summit seemed to be a disappointment, but now it is looked upon as the first step in a new stage of détente which led to a much greater understanding between the superpowers.

The next summit, at Reykjavik, would be more dramatic. Held almost a year after Geneva, on October 11-12, 1986, Reagan and Gorbachev met once again in the Icelandic capital. The summit had actually been postponed on several occasions, with tensions remaining high between the superpowers despite the warmer relationship of the two leaders at Geneva. Finally, a meeting was set and the pair met at another chilly location in a relatively neutral country. This time the conversations moved into a much deeper and serious direction. Reagan expressed his dislike of nuclear weapons, wanting to see them eradicated altogether and linking that belief to his SDI project. At this stage, Gorbachev did seem to outwit the older man, proposing that both sides decommission all nuclear weapons within 10 years, the so-called "zero option."[48] Shocked, Reagan agreed that this was in fact a good idea, one that he could support.

The proposal to completely remove all nuclear weapons disturbed advisors on both sides, and a counterproposal was agreed that would eliminate all but 100 nuclear weapons on each side. The

---

[46] CNN, *Cold War* (TV Series, produced by Jeremy Isaacs and Pat Mitchell, 1998)
[47] William Taubman, *Gorbachev: His Life and Times*. New York City: Simon and Schuster, 2017), p. 304.
[48] Tom Wicker, "The Zero Option Revived," *The New York Times*, 4 March 1987, https://www.nytimes.com/1987/03/04/opinion/in-the-nation-the-zero-option-revived.html, [accessed 22 May 2019]

idea received the support of Secretary of State George Shultz, and the summit appeared to be heading for a historic conclusion until Gorbachev pursued the SDI issue as a prerequisite of any agreement. Differences then emerged, and Reagan introduced a number of the West's criticisms of the Soviet Union since the previous period of détente, including human rights, the right of Soviet Jews to emigrate, and the war in Afghanistan. Gorbachev wanted SDI to be shelved, a condition Reagan would not countenance. As a result, the talks broke down and Reagan and Gorbachev left Reykjavik without a deal. More progress had been made for sure, but anything more concrete was proving elusive.[49] The Soviets were initially disappointed at the outcome of Reykjavik, but Gorbachev and Shevardnadze soon realized that they were on the cusp of something substantial if they could find a way through the obstacles on view at Reykjavik.

**Shultz**

The fallout for Reagan appeared to be more challenging than for Gorbachev. A furious Margaret Thatcher flew almost straightaway to Camp David, the presidential retreat, to berate Reagan over his proposed stance on nuclear disarmament. Thatcher was committed to the longstanding policy of nuclear deterrence and was disturbed that Reagan had been apparently

---

[49] CNN, *Cold War* (TV Series, produced by Jeremy Isaacs and Pat Mitchell, 1998)

close to ditching the core strategy of the Western alliance.

A month later, Reagan faced the biggest crisis of his Presidency: Iran Contra. In November 1986, it emerged that the US had secretly sold weapons to Iran - then a mortal American foe - and used the proceeds to fund the anti-communist forces in Nicaragua, where Congress had prohibited military support. Reagan survived the scandal, but it dogged him for the rest of his term.

Meanwhile, Gorbachev was visited in March 1987 by Thatcher, who was received warmly both by the Soviet leader and the crowds. Very unusually for a communist regime, Thatcher was allowed to participate in a television debate, during which she made the case for the superiority of the capitalist, democratic system. She also visited a church at a time when organized religion was not encouraged in the Soviet Union, and she had an open discussion with Gorbachev himself. Thatcher questioned the plan that had been tabled at Reykjavik on nuclear disarmament, saying that this would simply see a return of conventional warfare. As was her way during this period of the Cold War, she also met with well-known dissidents such as Sakharov.[50]

As had been the case at their 1984 meeting in Britain, the two leaders debated matters in a robust and - according to Thatcher's official biographer Charles Moore - even rude fashion.[51] Nevertheless, it appears that Gorbachev had no qualms rigorously arguing with Western world leaders and ending these conversations with his respect for his opponent heightened. It was a highly unusual visit and further evidence that the Soviet Union was changing rapidly.

It was perhaps surprising that Thatcher and Gorbachev developed such a good relationship given some of the events taking place behind the scenes. The streets and backstreets of Europe had long been the setting for espionage in the Cold War, and in the early years of the conflict it seemed that the best-known "double agents" worked for Moscow. However, the opposite trend emerged in the 1980s, and one of the biggest spy coups during this period was the identification of Oleg Gordievsky as a double agent working for Britain. Having joined the KGB in 1963 at the age of 25, Gordievsky, who became disenchanted with his country after the 1968 invasion of Czechoslovakia, was turned in the mid-1970s and provided intelligence to the British for a full 10 years.[52] Indeed, it was Gordievsky's intelligence that helped defuse the 1983 crisis over Operation Able Archer. At the time working in London, Gordievsky was essentially discovered by the KGB in May 1985, just after Gorbachev had become General Secretary, and recalled to Moscow for interrogation.[53] The British and Gordievsky hatched an escape plan and, astonishingly, managed to spirit the spy across the Finnish border, flying him to Britain on July

---

[50] Margaret Thatcher, *The Downing Street Years* (Harper Collins, 1993), p. 481.
[51] Charles Moore, *Margaret Thatcher The Authorized Biography: Volume Two Everything She Wants* (Allen Lane, 2015), p. 623.
[52] Charles Moore, *Margaret Thatcher The Authorized Biography: Volume Two Everything She Wants* (Allen Lane, 2015), p. 115.
[53] Charles Moore, *Margaret Thatcher The Authorized Biography: Volume Two Everything She Wants* (Allen Lane, 2015), p. 263.

22, 1985.[54]

The British kept the news of Gordievsky's defection quiet for several weeks - the Soviets believed Gordievsky had committed suicide - until late August, when Thatcher informed Gorbachev. It can be safely assumed that the KGB was not happy about the news that one of their spies had been working for the West for a decade, but, as was their style, they stayed busy attempting to drive a wedge between London and Washington on nuclear testing and muddy the waters of the Gordievsky situation. The following month, the news of Gordievsky's defection became public, and in the ensuing war of words both sides expelled 25 nationals stationed in the opposite country.[55] It was an example of how the Cold War was still fully operational.

Meanwhile, the conflict in Afghanistan continued. Gorbachev was intent on withdrawing from a war he had never supported, and he attempted to transfer the responsibility for prosecuting the war to the Afghans themselves, with mixed results. By 1987, Gorbachev was actively looking for some kind of accord so that his forces could completely withdraw, which he did between 1987 and 1989. The war had been a propaganda disaster and was another reason the Americans could heavily criticize the Soviets at superpower summits. By making progress on ending the war, Gorbachev believed he might be in a stronger position on the broader geopolitical level.

**An Acceleration of Domestic Policies**

Early on, Gorbachev had introduced some policies marking a break with the past, but the results had not been what he hoped. Certainly, Glasnost allowed a level of dissent previously unheard of in the Soviet Union, and this more liberal approach to politics was a breath of fresh air in both the USSR and its satellite states in Central and Eastern Europe, but Perestroika had done little to revive the Soviet economy. In many areas the situation was grim. Ordinary Soviet citizens had to wait in queues for hours to get hold of even rudimentary items of food. Consumer goods were rare and choice was non-existent. Such was the economic slump in mid-late 1980s' Soviet Union. Moreover, the centrally planned economy suppressed the kind of prices signalling normal in a market economy. This manifested itself in a communist economy as shortages. It also meant that if the price mechanism was introduced, the economic situation would become much worse before it normalized, which is indeed what happened in the early 1990s. Problems were already visible by the end of 1987, and hardliners were becoming increasingly concerned about Glasnost and Perestroika, as well as foreign policy.

Gorbachev, however, had sufficient power to continue to make bold reforms, so Glasnost continued apace, even as the openness he had encouraged now fatally threatened the integrity of the Soviet Union itself.[56] The permissive environment of discussion allowed Soviet citizens to air

---

[54] Charles Moore, *Margaret Thatcher The Authorized Biography: Volume Two Everything She Wants* (Allen Lane, 2015), p. 263.

[55] Charles Moore, *Margaret Thatcher The Authorized Biography: Volume Two Everything She Wants* (Allen Lane, 2015), p. 265.

their grievances, and many of these cut to the core of the system. As historian Vladislav Zubok put it, Glasnost "discredited the entire foundation of Soviet foreign policy and the regime itself."[57] Gorbachev believed the criticism of his domestic policies was a sign he was not being radical enough. As a result, he pressed on further with Glasnost and Perestroika, and he sought to reform the structures of the communist party.

After decades of being repressed and silenced, Glasnost suddenly allowed Soviet citizens to speak their mind. For many, when they looked back on the period, this was the key change: the fear to speak out evaporated under Gorbachev's rule.[58] This began to show itself in unexpected ways. Riots had broken out in Kazakhstan in 1987, and Gorbachev interpreted the unrest to unresolved questions of nationality within the Soviet Union and sought to bring in some accountability, even democracy, to the political structures of his enormous country.[59] Unfortunately for Gorbachev, his approach did not go nearly far enough, which meant his changes would offer the prospect of more political power without really delivering. Nationalist demonstrations, independence movements, and even ethnic tensions in multiethnic countries like Yugoslavia would worsen during the following years, playing a major role in the dissolution of the USSR.

Part of Gorbachev's Perestroika had been the concept of *Uskoreniye,* or "acceleration." Essentially another slogan, Uskoreniye vaguely set out how Soviet industry needed to improve its processes, increase productivity, and generally modernize. However, in a sign that everything was not proceeding as intended, Gorbachev phased out Uskoreniye at the Communist Party Plenum of June 1987, instead refocusing his energy on a revamped Perestroika. In Gorbachev's view, the Soviet economy required more restructuring rather than acceleration, but this nuance was lost on many observers within the Soviet Union itself.

At the end of 1987, dissent from within the party came out into the open and a power struggle for the heart and soul of Soviet communism began. A leading figure in the army, General Dmitry Yazov, started criticizing Gorbachev's approach, claiming that the Soviet leader was damaging the prestige and honor of the country. The pressure from hardliners like Yazov and sympathetic members of the Politburo would increase until the failed coup of August 1991. Perhaps even more insidious became the pressure from liberal nationalist reformers, most notably Boris Yeltsin.

From the vantage point of the early 1980s, Gorbachev was a radical leader who found himself increasingly criticized by conservatives and liberals, the former for going too far, the latter for

---

[56] Vladislav M. Zubok, *Failed Empire: The Soviet Union in the Cold War from Stalin to Gorbachev* (The University of North Carolina Press, 2007), p. 309.
[57] Vladislav M. Zubok, *Failed Empire: The Soviet Union in the Cold War from Stalin to Gorbachev* (The University of North Carolina Press, 2007), p. 309.
[58] CNN, *Cold War* (TV Series, produced by Jeremy Isaacs and Pat Mitchell, 1998)
[59] Stephen White, *Communism and its Collapse* (Routledge, 2002), p. 77.

not going far enough. The liberals' most significant voice within the ruling elite was Boris Yeltsin, a Russian who came to represent a common trend within communist countries. Yeltsin wanted greater accountability, democracy, and reform, and in communist terms he was a liberal. When these principles were implemented, however, they often morphed into nationalist demands. Greater representation and nationalism were the forces that ultimately spelled doom for the Soviet Union.

Yeltsin had been appointed Mayor of Moscow in late 1985 and the following year was promoted to Politburo candidacy status itself. Shortly afterwards, Yeltsin began to criticize the Gorbachev regime for its lack of tangible reform. His key demand was more democratic accountability within the structures of the communist system.

Frustrated by the lack of progress, Yeltsin resigned from his positions and challenged Gorbachev at the Party Plenum in October 1987. The usually drab, tightly-managed plenum saw extraordinary scenes as Yeltsin took the stage to berate Gorbachev, who stood stunned close by. Gorbachev subsequently attacked Yeltsin's "immaturity" and took the opportunity to deepen his criticism at a party meeting in November, days after Yeltsin had been hospitalized. Yeltsin was demoted but would take his revenge on Gorbachev after the General Secretary had put in motion some of Yeltsin's actual demands.

**Yeltsin**

Tensions increased in the republics during this second phase of Gorbachev's leadership, and many of these disputes would culminate in civil wars as the USSR disintegrated and left a power vaccuum. One of the first to break out into the open was between the republics of Armenia and Azerbaijan. The focal point of the animosity between the two republics was the territory of Nagorno-Karabakh, then an autonomous "Oblast" within Azerbaijan. The population of Nagorno-Karabakh was mixed, with a majority of ethnic Armenians. Intoxicated by the new openness in the Soviet Union, the parliament of Nagorno-Karabakh voted to join the Armenian Soviet Republic in February 1988.[60] This set in motion a series of events that led to full-scale war, one that has still not been fully resolved.

The Azerbaijani regime fiercely resisted the move, requesting Moscow step in to reverse the decision, and ethnic violence took place between Armenians and Azerbaijanis as border clashes worsened.[61] Gorbachev sent in the Soviet army to put down the fighting, but even that ultimately failed. It was an extreme example of how a seemingly positive development, Glasnost, had lifted the lid on destructive sentiments such as nationalism, leading to the kind of ethnic violence that had not been seen for most of the USSR's existence.

Unrest emerged around the same time in the republics of Georgia, Ukraine, and Belarus, as well as the Baltic republics of Latvia, Lithuania, and Estonia. Moscow struggled to exert its will over the republics' increasingly angry populations.

Gorbachev believed he could circumvent these problems by providing more of a pressure valve for the grievances let loose by Glasnost. His major democratic reform was the establishment of the Congress of People's Deputies. Gorbachev secured party support for the Congress in July 1988 and went into action the following year. Over 2,000 deputies would sit in the Congress which would appoint key decision-making bodies for the USSR, such as the Supreme Soviet.

Although truly democratic, the Congress was nevertheless a huge departure from previous Soviet practice. Candidates for deputies were selected as members of public organizations, but there was some room for actual choice, which was unheard of in the USSR. Significantly, not all the candidates were Communist Party members, and perhaps even more significantly, the Congress elections permitted figures such as Boris Yeltsin to run, allowing him to make a major comeback. As a result of his election, Yeltsin was chosen by the Congress to take a seat on the Supreme Soviet, which was now the ultimate decision-making body of the USSR. This would bring Yeltsin back into direct confrontation with Gorbachev.

**Crumbling Communism**

Gorbachev and Reagan met again in Washington in December 1987, but a fundamental shift had taken place between the Reykjavik and Washington summits. Gorbachev's team had reason

---

[60] Thomas De Waal, *Black Garden: Armenia and Azerbaijan Through Peace and War* (CAP, 2003)
[61] Thomas De Waal, *Black Garden: Armenia and Azerbaijan Through Peace and War* (CAP, 2003)

to doubt the SDI would amount to much, and what had seemed so critical at the first two Reagan-Gorbachev meetings now appeared to be less important. The Soviets believed - rightly as it turned out - that SDI was little more than a bluff. Believing this, however, did not change the fact that Moscow desperately wanted to reduce its military spending and reduce its nuclear commitments.[62] Gorbachev knew that in this endeavour he had a willing partner in Reagan.

The result of the summit was the INF (Intermediate-Range Nuclear Forces) Treaty, which banned land-based short and medium range nuclear missiles, but not those launched by air or sea. A joint task force was established, and over the space of the next months and years, both sides did decommission thousands of these cruise missiles. It was a high point of the Reagan-Gorbachev collaboration.

For Gorbachev, the Washington trip was a resounding success and showed incontrovertibly that he was a completely different kind of Soviet leader. As his motorcade sped through downtown Washington, the Soviet leader spotted a waving crowd. Inexplicably for a communist leader, usually unaccustomed to public discussion, Gorbachev asked his driver to stop his car so that he could meet some of the crowd. Smiling, waving, and shaking hands, the Soviet Union was suddenly embodied by a personable, reasonable person. The stunt enhanced Gorbachev's status both in the United States and back at home, and the tension of the Cold War appeared to have been taken down several notches literally overnight. Gorbachev met a number of American journalists and even businesspeople on his trip, including a prominent New York real estate magnate named Donald Trump.[63]

After the 1987 summit, the USSR and US entered what can be considered a second era of détente. Tensions between the superpowers had significantly decreased, nuclear weapons were being decommissioned, and relations between the leaderships were warm. In fact, Gorbachev spent 1988 going further than the Americans could ever have imagined in reducing Cold War tensions. Reagan visited Moscow in 1988 shortly before leaving office, and at one point he was asked whether he still thought the Soviet Union was an "Evil Empire." As he said no, he put his arm around a beaming Gorbachev.[64]

Over the course of 1988, Gorbachev put in motion what came to be known as the "Sinatra Doctrine," which meant the countries in the Soviet Bloc would be able to choose their own path, and do things "their way."[65] In a sign of how Gorbachev had fundamentally misread the feelings of most of the people in the communist world, he thought that introducing democracy into these states, including his own, would present few problems because they would happily choose a

---

[62] CNN, *Cold War* (TV Series, produced by Jeremy Isaacs and Pat Mitchell, 1998)
[63] Maureen Dowd, "As 'Gorby' Works the Crowd, Backward Reels the K.G.B.," *The New York Times*, 11 December 1987, https://www.nytimes.com/1987/12/11/world/the-summit-as-gorby-works-the-crowd-backward-reels-the-kgb.html, [accessed 22 May 2019]
[64] CNN, *Cold War* (TV Series, produced by Jeremy Isaacs and Pat Mitchell, 1998)
[65] *The Irish Times*, "How Berlin's Wall came tumbling down," 1 November 1999, https://www.irishtimes.com/news/how-berlin-s-wall-came-tumbling-down-1.245060, [accessed 23 May 2019]

socialist system and socialist parties of their own volition.[66] This culminated in a famous speech Gorbachev made to the United Nations General Assembly on December 8, 1988. Gorbachev, even by his standards, shocked the world by announcing that he would withdraw many - although not all - Soviet troops from Central and Eastern Europe.[67] He also asserted that Moscow would not interfere in the domestic affairs of these communist states.[68] Gorbachev vowed to "expand the Soviet Union's participation in the United Nations and Conference of Security and Cooperation in Europe human rights monitoring arrangements," and that "implementation of agreements on human rights should be binding on all states."[69] This was quite a departure for the leader of an authoritarian, communist state.

In *Gorbachev and the German Question: Soviet-West German Relations, 1985-1990*, author David Shumaker argued that Hungary's leaders, though desirous of encouraging a thaw, consistently communicated with Moscow, asking permission even as late as the summer of 1989 as to what to do about the thousands of East Germans fleeing the country through Hungary's borders.[70] Additionally, Shumaker notes, if the Soviet Union desired in any way to stop the crescendoing protest movement, Gorbachev could have used force or declaration of martial law to do so, even as late as 1989. Shumaker concluded, "Did the Soviet leader labor under the grand illusion of communism's inevitable triumph in Eastern Europe? Or alternatively, had Gorbachev already accepted the SED's imminent and total failure? In all likelihood, Gorbachev's reasoning lay somewhere between these two extremes."[71]

Around the same time, Gorbachev also negotiated an end to the war in Afghanistan, having wound down the conflict gradually since his rise to power. Before his speech to the UN, an agreement was reached in Geneva on April 14, 1988. Soviet Foreign Minister Shevardnadze signed the accords that ended the conflict, along with signatories from Afghanistan and Pakistan as well as US Secretary of State George Shultz.[72] The Soviets began pulling out their troops from Afghanistan in May 1988, taking until February 1989 to withdraw the last of its military.[73]

---

[66] CNN, *Cold War* (TV Series, produced by Jeremy Isaacs and Pat Mitchell, 1998)
[67] *History*, "Perestroika and Glasnost," 21 August 2018, https://www.history.com/topics/cold-war/perestroika-and-glasnost, [accessed 23 May 2019]
[68] *The New York Times*, "The Gorbachev Visit; Excerpts From Speech to U.N. on Major Soviet Military Cuts," 8 December 1988, https://www.nytimes.com/1988/12/08/world/the-gorbachev-visit-excerpts-from-speech-to-un-on-major-soviet-military-cuts.html, [accessed 23 May 2019}
[69] *The New York Times*, "The Gorbachev Visit; Excerpts From Speech to U.N. on Major Soviet Military Cuts," 8 December 1988, https://www.nytimes.com/1988/12/08/world/the-gorbachev-visit-excerpts-from-speech-to-un-on-major-soviet-military-cuts.html, [accessed 23 May 2019}
[70] David H. Shumaker, Gorbachev and the German Question: Soviet-West German Relations, 1985-1990 (Westport, CT: Praeger Publishers, 1995), 105, https://www.questia.com/read/27983284.
[71] Ibid 107.
[72] Rosanne Klass, "Afghanistan: The Accords," *Foreign Affairs*, 1988, https://www.foreignaffairs.com/articles/asia/1988-06-01/afghanistan-accords, [accessed 23 May 2019]
[73] Franz-Stefan Gady, "30-Year Anniversary of Soviet Withdrawal From Afghanistan: A Successful Disengagement Operation?," *The Diplomat*, 6 February 2019, https://thediplomat.com/2019/02/30-year-anniversary-of-soviet-withdrawal-from-afghanistan-a-successful-disengagement-operation/, [accessed 23 May 2019]

This marked another successful initiative for Gorbachev, but the country had been devastated by a decade of war and was divided into numerous factions. Fighting resumed shortly after the Soviet withdrawal, and after years of further conflict, the Taliban came to power in 1996, providing refuge for the al-Qaeda terrorist group. Both the Taliban and al-Qaeda had some connections with the US-funded mujahideen fighting the Soviets in the 1980s. Scholars used the term "blowback" to describe the long-term impact of the Cold War into the 2000s after the US and its allies invaded Afghanistan in the wake of the 9/11 attacks.[74]

Nevertheless, all these moves seemed to that Gorbachev was a man who stuck by his commitments and was someone keen to reduce the tension and proxy conflicts of the Cold War. He visited a number of communist states in 1989, encouraging their leaders to follow his lead on Glasnost and Perestroika. He was known to find a couple of these particularly frustrating, such as Romania's dictator Nicolae Ceaușescu and East German communist leader Erich Honecker. Gorbachev was apparently shocked by the dire state of Romania, with its paucity of goods and the desperate state of its people.[75] He also visited China in May 1989 to mend relations with Beijing after decades of tension during the Sino-Soviet split, and he became the first Soviet leader to visit China for almost 30 years. Nevertheless, his visit coincided with the Tiananmen Square student protests, which were violently crushed after Gorbachev left.

Gorbachev's openness meant that he would go so far as to entertain criticism of his East German ally from a West Germen leader, in the case of a conversation held between him and Helmut Kohl of West Germany in June of 1989. Kohl complained to Gorbachev, "Now a couple of words about our mutual friends. I will tell you directly that Erich Honecker concerns me a great deal. His wife has just made a statement, in which she called on East German youth to take up arms and, if necessary, defend the achievements of socialism against external enemies. She clearly implied that socialist countries which implement reforms, stimulate democratic processes, and follow their own original road, are enemies. Primarily, she had Poland and Hungary in mind."[76]

---

[74] Chalmers Johnson, *Blowback: The Costs and Consequences of American Empire*, (Holt, 2004)
[75] Celestine Bohlen, 'Gorbachev challenged by Romania', *The Washington Post*, 28 May 1987, https://www.washingtonpost.com/archive/politics/1987/05/28/gorbachev-challenged-by-romania/39020705-b8eb-470c-9244-e98f4257ce97/?utm_term=.823b4c8dafb3, [accessed 14 November 2018]
[76] William Taubman and Svetlana Savranskaya, "Chapter 3: If a Wall Fell in Berlin and Moscow Hardly Noticed, Would It Still Make a Noise?," in The Fall of the Berlin Wall: The Revolutionary Legacy of 1989, ed. Jeffrey A. Engel (New York: Oxford University Press, 2009), 85, https://www.questia.com/read/121390201.

**Kohl in 1989**

The Soviet leader also had an uncomfortable meeting with the Warsaw Pact leaders later that year. Changes were happening rapidly in Central and Eastern Europe by mid-1989, and a peaceful transition to liberal democracy appeared to be taking place in Hungary and Poland. This seriously concerned the likes of Honecker and Ceaușescu, who wanted Gorbachev to intervene and w worried the demand for reform would spread to their countries. This proved to be correct, and it had much deeper ramifications than anyone could have imagined.

Just a few short and hectic months later, Gorbachev would head to East Germany to visit his and Chancellor Kohl's "mutual friends". On October 6-7, 1989, East Berlin was to celebrate the 40th anniversary of the founding of the East German state, but security and surveillance by the Stasi had been increased heavily in response to Honecker's concerns that the visit of the Soviet leader, Gorbachev could cause unrest in the city. Gorbachev's very controlled visit did spark local protests, though he did not openly call for reform in a way that would make the East German leadership uncomfortable. He did, however, in his meeting with the leaders of the Socialist party give a warning that "one cannot overlook signals of reality. Life punishes those who arrive too late. We have learned this from our development".[77] Shumaker argues, though, that Gorbachev did the most he could to make the point that he supported national sovereignty: "During his stay in East Berlin for the 40th anniversary of the East German state, Gorbachev

---

[77] Gorbachev qtd. in Shumaker 112.

publicly stressed that 'in each country the people will determine what they need and what to do'."[78]  Behind the scenes, Honecker defended his hard line attitude to Gorbachev, reminding him that the East Germans boasted a higher standard of living than the citizens of the Soviet Union. If East Germany lost the ability to retain its young people, Honecker warned, East Germany's reputation and her high-tech generation would be lost to unrest and exodus.

According to Valery Boldin, a former Gorbachev aide, when Gorbachev returned from East Germany, he "announced that Honecker's days were numbered and that we should start thinking about the reunification of Germany".[79]  On October 16th, Egon Krenz and two other East German leaders, Willi Stoph and Erich Mielke, wrote to Moscow seeking Gorbachev's permission to replace Honecker as leader. Honecker would be removed from office only a few days later.[80]

Observers in the Soviet Union described Gorbachev's approach to the situation in Europe as "ad hoc". According to observers, Gorbachev and his minister of Soviet affairs were "[a]ble but inexperienced, impatient to reach agreement, but excessively self-assured and flattered by the Western media… often outwitted and outplayed by their Western partners".[81] History records no direct comment on the fall of the wall by Gorbachev, whose own aides found him unable to be reached by phone on the night of November 9th. That said, in 2009, 20 years after the Wall fell Gorbachev did make comments to Western reporters about the Berlin Wall: "If the Soviet Union did not want [the wall to fall], nothing would have happened, not any kind of unification." When asked what the alternative would be, Gorbachev answered, "I don't know, maybe a World War III…I am very proud of the decision we made. The wall did not simply fall, it was destroyed, just as the Soviet Union was destroyed…The fall of the Berlin Wall was a synthesized indication of what was going on in the world and where it was heading to. My policy was open and sincere, a policy aimed at using democracy and not spilling blood, but this cost me very [dearly], I can tell you that."[82]

When Gorbachev decided it was time for Honecker to exit the scene, the Politburo had already decided on his replacement, a younger man, to be sure, but a man embroiled in the same fight as his unfortunate predecessor. Egon Krenz had grown up in the Soviet system, attending college and becoming known as the "crown prince" of the GDR for his faithfulness in matters of party security .[83] He replaced his mentor and friend Honecker, the man he called his "foster father and political teacher", after betraying him and voting for his ouster in the midst of Honecker's

---

[78] Ibid 106.
[79] Valery Boldin, Ten Years That Shook the World: The Gorbachev Era as Witnessed by His Chief of Staff, trans. Evelyn Rossiter (New York: Basic Books, 1994), 143,
[80] Large, 525.
[81] Vladislav M. Zubok, A Failed Empire: The Soviet Union in the Cold War from Stalin to Gorbachev (Chapel Hill, NC: University of North Carolina Press, 2007), 327,
[82] Marquardt, Alexander. "Gorbachev: The Man Who Prevented World War III?" *ABC News.com.* 8 November 2009.
[83] Dennis Kavanagh, ed., A Dictionary of Political Biography (Oxford: Oxford University Press, 1998), 276, https://www.questia.com

disagreements with the Soviets and failures to control the burgeoning protest movement in East Germany. Krenz, however, did not have the trust of the people any more than Honecker had at the end of his rule. An exiled East German said Krenz was "a walking invitation to flee the republic".[84] Stern calls Krenz "a less doctrinaire functionary [than Honecker] mouthing vague notions of reform".[85]

Krenz, who unluckily received the ailing Honecker's "blessing" upon his exit, proved paralyzed and unable to deal with the demands for reform. Krenz lost popularity by taking over not only as the Socialist party leader but also as head of state, the same position which Honecker had occupied.[86] Despite Krenz's desperate attempts to placate reformers in East Germany, his promises proved too little, too late. He was seen as nothing more than Honecker "with a gallbladder", as the joke went. The number of protestors in Leipzig grew during Krenz's first six weeks in power from 70,000 to over half a million, and Krenz opened the borders with Czechoslovakia on the advice of the Soviets only after he revealed to Gorbachev the extreme amount of debt East Germany had incurred with the West. Krenz and Gorbachev knew they would need to build good will with the West in order to make the payments necessary for the GR to survive.[87]

Finally, tensions between East Germany and her resentful neighbors had reached a breaking point. With literally tens of thousands of East German refugees clogging the streets, highways, and embassies of her neighbor nations, it was up to East Germany to ease travel restrictions and make some concessions to stem the tide, so the decision was made to allow travel outside of East Berlin for one month to those with proper passports. Large notes that the number of East Germans with proper passports was so low that this would not have caused a high influx of travel outside of the borders. However, the hastily called press conference and the rewriting of the policy up to the last hour meant that a mistake would be made that would change the world as the Germans knew it.

Guenter Schabowski was the official spokesperson at a press conference that was being televised live throughout East Germany. Charged with delivering the new travel guidelines in a hastily-called press conference, Schabowski began his remarks: "You see, comrades, I was informed today…that such an announcement had been…distributed earlier today. You should actually have it already…1) 'Applications for travel abroad by private individuals can now be made without the previously existing requirements (of demonstrating a need to travel or proving familial relationships). The travel authorizations will be issued within a short time. Grounds for denial will only be applied in particular exceptional cases. The responsible departments of passport and registration control in the People's Police district offices in the GDR are instructed

---

[84] Ibid. 526.
[85] Stern 457.
[86] Kavanagh 276.
[87] Vladislav M. Zubok, A Failed Empire: The Soviet Union in the Cold War from Stalin to Gorbachev (Chapel Hill, NC: University of North Carolina Press, 2007), 326

to issue visas for permanent exit without delays and without presentation of the existing requirements for permanent exit.""

After being asked when it would come into effect, Schabowski replied, "That comes into effect, according to my information, immediately, without delay." When asked if it also applies for West Berlin, he responded, "Permanent exit can take place via all border crossings from the GDR to the FRG and West Berlin, respectively."[88]

**Picture of the press conference**

*The Wall Street Journal* speculated that Schabowski had faltered not because he had not prepared carefully enough, as some charged, but because he was "not used to scrutiny by a free press…[And] he couldn't deal with rapid-fire questions from international journalists".[89] Whatever the real cause of Schabowski's struggle to communicate, it became immediately clear that "seeming accidents have the power to shape history".[90] Later, American journalist Tom Brokaw would recall following Schakowsky upstairs after the conference had concluded and

---

[88] Guenter Schabowski, "Guenter Schabowski's Press Conference in the GDR International Press Center," Making the History of 1989, Item #449, http://chnm.gmu.edu/1989/items/show/449 (accessed February 27 2015, 8:28 pm).

[89] Walker, Marcus. "Did Journalists' Questions Topple the Berlin Wall?" The Wall Street Journal. 7 November 2014.

[90] Stern 459.

asking him to re-read the portion of the brief that lifted the travel restrictions on border crossings between East and West Berlin directly. It was then, Brokaw realized, that the end of the Berlin Wall had come. In his newscast, he told the watching world, "This is a historic night…. The East German Government has just declared that East German citizens will be able to cross the wall … without restrictions."[91] Schabowski would be expelled from the party but fail to escape prosecution as a high Politburo official; he served only a few months of a three-year sentence after distancing himself from communist ideals.

On the evening of November 9, 1989, Harald Jaeger, an East German border guard, watched a television as he ate a meal at the canteen before arriving for his guard duty shift at the Berlin Wall that night at 6:00 p.m. Hearing the removal of travel restrictions would take place "immediately", he remembers "almost choking on my bread roll". He arrived at the wall to find other skeptical guards and made multiple telephone calls to his superiors, attempting to get clarification about what to do with the now gathering crowds. At first, Jaeger's superiors simply ignored his question, telling them to send people without authorization home. After realizing the seriousness of the situation, however, Jaeger was instructed to let the "most agitated" members of the crowd pass through to West Berlin in hopes of appeasing them. Obviously, the opposite effect was achieved and Jaeger had no further instruction from his superiors. Fearing for the safety of the burgeoning crowd, Jaeger delivered the order to open the border between East and West Berlin at 11:30 p.m.[92] Thus, Jaeger is most often credited with being the man who actually "took down" the Berlin Wall.

Another East German border guard, Erich Wittman, recalled his memory of the evening: "I was promoted to Corporal, and was directly posted as the Officer of the main checkpoint of the Berlin wall. I still remember the tensions, thousands of cars was in front of me, honking and wanted me to move, which I refused….The news of the Berlin wall being open for anyone hadn't reached us who were posted at the wall, only when my girlfriend, who I for the first time on [sic] months seen, came to me and told me about it. I was in shock and didn't know what to do, all around me, thousands of people started to gather around me, climbing over the wall, some even brought tools and sledge-hammers and started to destroy the wall, the people kept yelling at us as we told them to stay back, then…On the TV, which I saw through the window of the Guard's Resting place, I could see the politicians ordering the opening to West Berlin for everyone, I ordered the soldiers to open the gates and let the cars pass, the yells formed into cheers and all over us, people came to hug me and my men, and the cars kept swarming over the border. Erika grabbed onto my uniform, and pulled me to her, and hugged me, I responded in kissing her, then a camera man appeared on the scene and filmed the opening of the wall, and got us on tape…The supreme officer came to me later, asked me why the people are flooding over to West Germany,

---

[91] Melvyn P. Leffler, "Chapter 5: Dreams of Freedom, Temptations of Power," in The Fall of the Berlin Wall: The Revolutionary Legacy of 1989, ed. Jeffrey A. Engel (New York: Oxford University Press, 2009), 136,
[92] "Former border guard Harald Jaeger recalls how he opened the Berlin Wall." South China Morning Post. 6 November 2014.

I told him. The German Democratic Republic is dead, they announced it on Television, open your borders as well for these people. He quickly went away, and all over East Germany the news came, and the Berlin wall was flooded by people over several days."

**A crane removing pieces of the wall in December 1989**

Pictures of East Germans talking to West Germans through the wall in late November 1989

**1990 picture of the graffiti and pieces of the wall chipped away**

A New World Order

The world had been taken by surprise when the Berlin Wall came down, and Kohl wasted no time in asserting himself regarding the situation. On November 28, Kohl gave a speech setting out "Ten Points" that would lead to greater German cooperation, and eventually even reunification.[93] The concessions made in the 1972 Basic Treaty had apparently been forgotten, and the pre-1972 policy of incorporating the whole of Germany within one democratic state was

---

[93] The German Chancellery, 'The Federal Chancellor, Helmut Kohl; 1982-1998', [accessed 31 October 2017], https://www.bundeskanzlerin.de/Webs/BKin/EN/Chancellery/Timeline_Federal_Chancellors_since_1949/Kohl/kohl_node.html, Robert Hutchings, 'American Diplomacy and the End of the Cold War in Europe', *Foreign Policy Breakthroughs: Cases in Successful Diplomacy*, ed. Robert Hutchings and Jeremi Suri (Oxford: Oxford University Press, 2015, pp. 148-172), p. 160.

back on the table.

Though Kohl's objectives appeared ambitious, it was thought the Soviets would not accept a unified Germany as part of NATO, and two of West Germany's closest allies, Britain and France, were opposed to unification, fearing Germany might try to dominate Europe as it had attempted to do in the first half of the 20th century. Margaret Thatcher, in an interview outside 10 Downing Street, warned that talk of German reunification was much, much "too fast" and that East Germany would be required to show its development as a democracy before that could be taken under serious consideration. Despite issuing cautions about the pace at which reunification should take place and the idea that it was impossible for all East Germans to leave the country[94], Thatcher did take a moment to delight in the historical moment: "I think it is a great day for freedom. I watched the scenes on television last night and again this morning because I felt one ought not only hear about them but see them because you see the joy on people's faces and you see what freedom means to them; it makes you realize that you cannot stifle or suppress people's desire for liberty and so I watched with the same joy as everyone else."[95]

Meanwhile, President George H.W. Bush was determined to use American influence to bring a peaceful end to the Cold War and forge a durable, pro-Western settlement in Europe. He was assisted by the fact that his administration had good working relations with Gorbachev and other Soviet officials, such as Foreign Minister Shevardnadze. As a result, an environment of mutual trust, or at least good faith, existed between Moscow and Washington in 1990. The Bush administration also realized that Gorbachev was coming under increasing pressure from his own hardliners, as well as liberal reformers such as Boris Yeltsin and nationalist agitators in the Soviet republics.

The US was keen to support Gorbachev and prevent a chaotic breakup of the USSR, with the exception of the Baltic states (Latvia, Lithuania and Estonia), which had been incorporated into the Soviet Union at the end of the Second World War. Many of the people occupying the Baltic republics bitterly opposed Soviet rule, and as the communist regimes toppled in rapid succession in Europe, separatist movements saw their opportunity. The independence-minded populations in the Baltic republics formed "Popular Fronts" in the late 1980s, with Estonia declaring sovereignty in 1988 and Latvia and Lithuania following in the summer of 1989. In August 1989, protestors in the three republics formed a human chain across their territory, known as the "Baltic Way." The protest marked the 50th anniversary of the Hitler-Stalin pact non-aggression pact that prevented immediate hostilities between the Nazis and Soviets in the Second World War but set the Baltic countries on course for occupation by both dictatorships. On March 11, 1990, the Lithuanian parliament declared independence, drawing an uncertain response from Moscow. In the interim period, Latvia and Estonia also declared independence before the Red

---

[94] Thatcher, Margaret. "Remarks on the Berlin Wall (fall thereof)". Thatcher Archive: COI transcript. 10 November 1989.
[95] Ibid.

Army attempted, dramatically, to reassert Soviet sovereignty.

In one of the darkest moments of Gorbachev's premiership, he sent the Soviet army into Lithuania to take back control from the separatists in early 1991. Known as the "January Events," the Lithuanians resisted the Soviet army in the capital city, Vilnius. 14 Lithuanians died and 700 were injured before the Soviet army retreated, and Gorbachev was heavily criticized for the move. The Lithuanians, although overjoyed after having pushed back the Red Army, were furious with Gorbachev's actions, even as just about everyone understood the violence would have been far worse under a different Soviet leader.[96] It may be that Gorbachev finally saw the writing on the wall, that his country was facing an existential crisis, or that he had come under heavy pressure from military hawks and hardliners. Ultimately, though, the Soviets essentially conceded the independence of the Baltic states, and in a few short years they would be part of NATO and the EU.

Gorbachev experienced a strange duality in 1990 and 1991. He was feted on the international scene for his role in ending Soviet domination in Central and Eastern Europe and allowing these states to make a peaceful transition away from communism. The international arena was transformed, with the Soviet Union suddenly acting virtually in concert with the United States. At home, however, the USSR was in turmoil, and Gorbachev was apparently powerless to prevent his country's dissolution.

In August 1990, Iraqi dictator Saddam Hussein invaded tiny, oil-rich Kuwait, and President Bush quickly put together a broad-based coalition of countries with the goal of forcing the Iraqis out of Kuwait. Bush put pressure on Iraq and eventually obtained permission to use military force against the Iraqis through the United Nations Security Council. After months of sanctions, "Operation Desert Storm" achieved a quick victory against Hussein and forced the Iraqi forces from Kuwait in early 1991. Gorbachev acquiesced to a number of American resolutions in the UN throughout this time, most notably those on Iraq.[97]

The US and USSR also worked together on the Middle East peace process. Bush convened the Madrid Peace Conference in October and November 1991, an attempt to bring together the hostile parties in the Middle East and figure out a solution to the Palestinian-Israeli conflict. Gorbachev was in attendance and threw his support behind the process. Again, what was different about this move was that traditionally the US and Soviet Union had used the region as a proxy for their broader conflict. Various states and factions had received support from either the Americans or Soviets, and sometimes both. A united front from Bush and Gorbachev changed the calculus for many leaders in the region, not least the Israelis.

---

[96] Witold Janczys and Markian Ostaptschuk, "The January bloodbath in Lithuania 25 years on," *Deutsche Welle*, 13 January 2016, https://www.dw.com/en/the-january-bloodbath-in-lithuania-25-years-on/a-18876152, [accessed 24 May 2019]

[97] Graham E. Fuller, "Moscow and the Gulf War," *Foreign Affairs*, Summer 1991, https://www.foreignaffairs.com/articles/russia-fsu/1991-06-01/moscow-and-gulf-war, [accessed 24 May 2019]

Nevertheless, by late 1991 Gorbachev's authority was fading fast. Although still a statesman on the world stage, his own country was in turmoil. Georgians had taken to the streets in April 1989, demanding secession from the Soviet Union and the incorporation of the disputed territory of Abkhazia. Soviet troops cracked down on the demonstrators, killing 20 people. An anti-Georgian riot broke out in Abkhazia soon afterwards, marking the start of a conflict between Abkhazians and Georgians that would stretch into the 1990s.

A similar situation emerged in Moldova. The Romanian-speaking population agitated for independence from the USSR during 1989, and another "Popular Front" formed. Some Moldovans even wanted to join Romania itself. This was opposed, however, by the pro-Russian population in the eastern region of Transnistria, which led to another conflict that is still unresolved nearly 30 years later.

Nationalist demonstrations also broke out in Ukraine, Belarus, Kazakhstan, and Uzbekistan, and in several cases Moscow sent in troops to quell the disturbances. Azerbaijan's "Black January" came when Soviet troops attempted to retain control of the republic and in the process killed 130 people.

Six republics declared independence in 1990, including Moldova, Georgia, and Armenia, but it was clear the real danger to the integrity of the USSR would come if its largest republics - Russia and Ukraine - attempted to break away. Russia held its first democratic elections in June 1991, with Boris Yeltsin emerging victorious with 57% of the vote. The Soviet Union was a fragile edifice rapidly losing the consent of its constituent republics, and Russia now wanted to reformulate the USSR as a federation of independent states, loosening the grip of the Soviet Union.

In a final, desperate attempt to prevent the implosion of the USSR, a group of hardliners launched a coup. On August 19, 1991, the Soviet plotters - including Defense Minister Dmitry Yazov and KBG leader Vladimir Kryuchkov - visited Gorbachev at his holiday dacha in Crimea and attempted something along the same lines as in a previous era, such as the defenestration of Nikita Khrushchev in 1964. They told the 60-year-old Gorbachev that he would retire due to health reasons and then proceeded to make a preposterous announcement on Soviet television about a change of leadership.

The coup was clear for all to see. Boris Yeltsin stormed down to the Russian parliament, demanding the coup plotters step down and reinstate Gorbachev. The plotters blinked on August 21 upon realizing their takeover had little support either in the corridors of power or in the country at large.

Gorbachev was reinstated and back in office, but his power was almost gone. In the months after the coup, 10 former Soviet republics declared their independence, and a transitional confederation known as the Commonwealth of Independent States (CIS) was put in place, intending to allow a looser version of the Soviet Union to continue. This became a reality after a meeting between the leaders of Russia (Yeltsin), Ukraine (Leonid Kravchuk) and Belarus (Stanislav Shushkevich) on December 8, 1991. The so-called "Belovezha Accords," named after the location in Belarus where they were signed, effectively withdrew the three countries from the USSR and declared the Soviet Union dissolved.

There has been some debate as to whether the leaders had the authority to do this. After all, Gorbachev was still the head of the USSR, but nevertheless it was clear where real power now existed. Yeltsin was the most important political leader in the region after the failed August coup, and the accords would establish a new Russian Federation which he would lead until the end of the decade. Gorbachev initially rejected the assertions of the Belovezha Accords but quickly faced the new reality and yielded. On December 25, 1991, Gorbachev announced in a television address that he would resign and the Soviet Union would be dissolved at the end of the year. After 74 years of communist experiment, the Soviet Union was no more, and the Cold War was over.

It has often been said that Mikhail Gorbachev was far more popular in the West than in his native Russia. Having overseen the relatively peaceful end of the Cold War and domination of communism in Central and Eastern Europe, Gorbachev's domestic policies led remorselessly to the downfall of the Soviet Union itself. By 1992, the Soviet Union had been transformed into 15 independent states, and for most of these new states, the 1990s proved to be worse than the previous decade. Some experienced civil war, and breakaway provinces such as Chechnya went through bloody conflicts in their attempts to gain independence. Many of these conflicts are still unresolved.

The economies of these states were also heavily damaged. Prices soared while goods remained scarce, and Russia experienced a humiliating default and devaluation of the rouble currency in 1998. Many of these states continued in the authoritarian tradition, as democracy proved very difficult to embed. In the worst examples, former communist party bosses were effectively made autocrats for life. Resources were fiercely fought over during the 1990s - encouraged by liberals in the West, the former Soviet states implemented an unrestrained version of capitalism, with chaotic and mismanaged privatizations and economic reforms. The phenomenon of the ultra-rich "oligarch" emerged during this period, and ultimately, Vladimir Putin restored some semblance of order to Russia after he came to power in late 1999 and revived the Russian economy as the country benefitted from a commodity price boom.

How much of this legacy was due to the policies of the Gorbachev regime remains a much-debated question. Several of his reforms led to far-reaching, unpredictable consequences, and it is probably fair to say that most other Soviet leaders would not have relinquished the Warsaw Pact states without a fight in 1989. In this respect, Gorbachev's generally peaceable approach and his humane outlook allowed these upheavals to take place without as much bloodshed.

Of course, while those affected will be debating the rights and wrongs of Gorbachev's decisions for decades to come, what cannot be argued is the significance of his leadership.

**Online Resources**

Other books about 20th century history by Charles River Editors

Other books about Russian history by Charles River Editors

Other books about Gorbachev on Amazon

**Bibliography**

Christopher Andrew and Vasili Mitrokhin, *The Mitrokhin Archive: The KGB in Europe and the West*, (Gardners Books, 2000)

Edwin Bacon & Mark Sandle, *Brezhnev Reconsidered* (Palgrave Macmillan, 2002)

S.J. Ball, *The Cold War: An International History 1947-1991* (London: Arnold, 1998)

Celestine Bohlen, 'Gorbachev challenged by Romania', *The Washington Post*, 28 May 1987, https://www.washingtonpost.com/archive/politics/1987/05/28/gorbachev-challenged-by-romania/39020705-b8eb-470c-9244-e98f4257ce97/?utm_term=.823b4c8dafb3

Archie Brown, *The Gorbachev Factor* (Oxford University Press, 1996)

John Campbell, *Margaret Thatcher Volume Two: The Iron Lady* (Random House, 2003)

CNN, *Cold War* (TV Series, produced by Jeremy Isaacs and Pat Mitchell, 1998)

Thomas De Waal, *Black Garden: Armenia and Azerbaijan Through Peace and War* (CAP, 2003)

Maureen Dowd, "As 'Gorby' Works the Crowd, Backward Reels the K.G.B.," *The New York Times*, 11 December 1987, https://www.nytimes.com/1987/12/11/world/the-summit-as-gorby-works-the-crowd-backward-reels-the-kgb.html

Stan Fedun, 'How Alcohol Conquered Russia', *The Atlantic*, 25 September 2003, https://www.theatlantic.com/international/archive/2013/09/how-alcohol-conquered-russia/279965/

Graham E. Fuller, "Moscow and the Gulf War," *Foreign Affairs*, Summer 1991, https://www.foreignaffairs.com/articles/russia-fsu/1991-06-01/moscow-and-gulf-war

Mary Fulbrook, *History of Germany, 1918-2000: the divided nation* (Oxford: Blackwell, 2002)

Franz-Stefan Gady, "30-Year Anniversary of Soviet Withdrawal From Afghanistan: A Successful Disengagement Operation?," *The Diplomat*, 6 February 2019, https://thediplomat.com/2019/02/30-year-anniversary-of-soviet-withdrawal-from-afghanistan-a-successful-disengagement-operation/

The German Chancellery, 'The Federal Chancellor, Helmut Kohl; 1982-1998', [accessed 31 October 2017], https://www.bundeskanzlerin.de/Webs/BKin/EN/Chancellery/Timeline_Federal_Chancellors_since_1949/Kohl/kohl_node.html

Mark Gilbert, *Cold War Europe: The Politics of a Contested Continent* (Rowman & Littlefield, 2014)

*History*, "Perestroika and Glasnost," 21 August 2018, https://www.history.com/topics/cold-war/perestroika-and-glasnost

Godfrey Hodgson, *People's Century: From the dawn of the century to the eve of the millennium* (Godalming: BBC Books, 1998)

Robert Hutchings, 'American Diplomacy and the End of the Cold War in Europe', *Foreign Policy Breakthroughs: Cases in Successful Diplomacy*, ed. Robert Hutchings and Jeremi Suri (Oxford: Oxford University Press, 2015, pp. 148-172)

*The Irish Times*, "How Berlin's Wall came tumbling down," 1 November 1999, https://www.irishtimes.com/news/how-berlin-s-wall-came-tumbling-down-1.245060

Witold Janczys and Markian Ostaptschuk, "The January bloodbath in Lithuania 25 years on," *Deutsche Welle*, 13 January 2016, https://www.dw.com/en/the-january-bloodbath-in-lithuania-25-years-on/a-18976152

Chalmers Johnson, *Blowback: The Costs and Consequences of American Empire*, (Holt, 2004)

Rosanne Klass, "Afghanistan: The Accords," *Foreign Affairs*, 1988, https://www.foreignaffairs.com/articles/asia/1988-06-01/afghanistan-accords

Michael McFaul, *Russia's Unfinished Revolution: Political Change from Gorbachev to Putin* (Cornell University Press, 2002)

Charles Moore, *Margaret Thatcher The Authorized Biography: Volume Two Everything She Wants* (Allen Lane, 2015)

"The Gorbachev Visit; Excerpts From Speech to U.N. on Major Soviet Military Cuts," *The New York Times*, 8 December 1988, https://www.nytimes.com/1988/12/08/world/the-gorbachev-visit-excerpts-from-speech-to-un-on-major-soviet-military-cuts.html

Arkady Ostrovsky, *The Invention of Russia: The Journey from Gorbachev's Freedom to Putin's War* (Atlantic Books, 2015)

William Taubman, *Gorbachev: His Life and Times*. New York City: Simon and Schuster, 2017)

Margaret Thatcher, *The Downing Street Years* (Harper Collins, 1993)

William J. Tompson, *The Soviet Union under Brezhnev*, (Routledge, 2014).

Peter Wensierski, 'Die WG der Rebellen', *Der Spiegel*, 3 October 2014, http://www.spiegel.de/einestages/leipzig-wie-es-1989-zur-montagsdemonstration-kam-a-993513.html

Stephen White, *Communism and its Collapse* (Routledge, 2002)

Tom Wicker, "The Zero Option Revived," *The New York Times*, 4 March 1987, https://www.nytimes.com/1987/03/04/opinion/in-the-nation-the-zero-option-revived.html

Vladislav M. Zubok, *Failed Empire: The Soviet Union in the Cold War from Stalin to Gorbachev* (The University of North Carolina Press, 2007)

# Free Books by Charles River Editors

We have brand new titles available for free most days of the week. To see which of our titles are currently free, click on this link.

# Discounted Books by Charles River Editors

We have titles at a discount price of just 99 cents everyday. To see which of our titles are currently 99 cents, click on this link.

Manufactured by Amazon.ca
Bolton, ON